D1339494

FREDA PARKER

VICTORIANA

CROSS STITCH, EMBROIDERY AND PATCHWORK PROJECTS

BLITZ

Published by Blitz Editions
an imprint of Bookmart Limited
Registered Number 2372865
Trading as Bookmart Limited
Desford Road, Enderby, Leicester LE9 5AD

Text copyright © Freda Parker 1990, 1991, 1994
Charts copyright © Anaya Publishers Ltd 1990, 1991, 1994
Photographs copyright © Anaya Publishers Ltd 1990,
1991, 1994

All rights reserved. No part of this publication may be
reproduced, stored in a retrieval system, or
transmitted, in any form or by any means, electronic,
mechanical, photocopying, recording or otherwise,
without the permission of the copyright holder.

British Library Cataloguing in Publication Data
A catalogue record for this book is available from the
British Library

ISBN 1 85605 247 8

Typeset by RGM Associates, Southport
Printed and bound in China

CONTENTS

INTRODUCTION

The home was the centre of Victorian life. This was particularly true of the growing middle classes, who liked to fill their houses with furniture and bric-a-brac in the comfortable, crowded style that was typical of the period. The Victorian home often also combined an exuberant mixture of styles, including Gothic, Renaissance, Elizabethan and Eastern.

Furniture was rounded and very thickly padded. Strong colours, that might be considered gaudy today, were widely used and many different patterns were put together. Windows were heavily draped with as many as three layers of fabric for curtains and blinds, and with a decorative pelmet above. Mantelpieces, shelves, tables and the piano were also draped. Pictures covered the walls and every available surface had its share of ornaments.

For the working classes sewing was, of course, a practical necessity. It was a skill needed to make and mend around the home and perhaps to supplement a meagre income. For the middle and upper classes sewing played a different, but equally prominent role. Women from these classes had enough domestic help to leave them plenty of time on their hands. Paid employment was unthinkable for ladies, and very few girls were given an academic education. However, the Victorian work ethic deplored idleness, and so young ladies kept themselves busy with such refined accomplishments as drawing, painting, music, singing, dancing, and, of course, needlework. Their sewing would include making and repairing household items and producing garments for the poor, but the greatest part of their time was spent on embroidery and fancy work, including patchwork.

Victorian ladies embroidered a wide variety of articles for the home, including chair covers, firescreens, footstools, bell-pulls, table-covers, tie-backs and elaborate pelmets called lambrequins. Some personal items they worked - for example, album and prayerbook covers, pen wipers, blotters, watch pockets and cigar cases - are now obsolete. Numerous designs for embroidery were published in periodicals of the time.

The materials and fabrics used for embroidery in the Victorian period were varied, ranging from silk to leather. Even punched card was used to produce such creations as counted thread pictures and bookmarks. Threads were of wool, cotton and silk in different types and weights. Silk was more readily available than it is now. Gold and silver threads were popular also, as was ribbon. In addition there were more eccentric materials such as straw, fish scales, feathers and beetles' wings sometimes incorporated into the work.

Then, as now, there were basically two different types of patchwork made — with or without papers. With the first, the 'English method', small geometric shapes which had previously been basted to thin card were oversewn together. Often a single shape was used to cover a whole bedcover in a repeat pattern. Sometimes two or more shapes were combined to give yet more patterns. It was not usual for this type of patchwork to be quilted, and the fabrics used were often luxurious silks and velvets.

With the second type of patchwork, the 'American method', the patches were seamed together with running stitches. Shapes were usually simple squares, rectangles and triangles, and might be quite large. This type of work was normally quilted, and was the method of piecing most commonly used in the United States of America, but was also popular in the North of England, Wales and Ireland. A third method of patchwork is to apply the patches to a backing fabric, as with Log Cabin, a very popular technique in the Victorian era.

The concept of this book spans the Victorian period and covers a wide variety of needlework and patchwork techniques. The aim is to present a selection of projects that will give a taste of the most characteristic types of needlecraft from this rich and fertile era.

Many of the threads and fabrics popular in Victorian times are no longer available, so there are suggested modern alternatives that will give an authentic look. There is also an emphasis on designs suited to the modern lifestyle, which has meant avoiding pen-wipers, cigar cases and embroidered braces in favour of more useful items such as cushions, bedlinen, a footstool, throws and bedcovers. Also included are cross stitch samplers, pictures and boxes. In a more frivolous vein, there is a pattern for one of the most typical of all Victorian projects - a pair of Berlin woolwork slippers.

BEADWORK

Beads featured widely in Victorian embroidery. Millions of them were sold and they were used to decorate garments, to trim braids or to decorate footstools, cushions and fire-screens. They were even used to cover piano stools, which must have been rather uncomfortable. Beads were incorporated into knitting and crochet and were made up into fringes for lampshades and bags. In short, they were used to decorate almost anything from watch pockets and braces to tea cosies and valances.

Beadwork requires an enormous number of beads. The tiny purse shown on page 15 took about 1,200, and the footstool (opposite) required 8,000 for the background alone.

For bead embroidery the beads were either sewn by hand or they were tamboured. Tambouring involves holding the fabric taut in a frame and using a fine hook, rather like a crochet hook, to work the stitches. For beadwork on canvas the beads were sewn on with either tent stitch or half cross stitch and designs were worked from charts similar to those used for Berlin woolwork. A piece might be worked entirely in beads, or wool was sometimes used for the background. Alternatively, the design might be mainly Berlin woolwork with beads used simply for highlights.

The beads required for beadwork are readily available today and are generally sold in boxes of approximately 600. Within each box there will be slight variations in the size of bead, but this will not affect the finished work. When working on canvas, make sure that the size of the bead matches the mesh of the canvas. If the beads are too large for the canvas holes they

Opposite: Beadwork footstools sometimes took thousands of tiny beads to complete. Flowers were a favourite subjects of Victorian embroiderers, and used for every type of embroidery.

will force the threads out of alignment and will not lie neatly.

Most types of beadwork require a beading needle. This is a particularly fine and flexible needle with a narrow eye, enabling it to pass easily through the hole in the bead. There are different thicknesses of needle to suit different sizes of bead but because of their narrow eyes, they are difficult to thread. It helps to wax the thread, by drawing it over a piece of candle or beeswax. It is a good idea not to cut off a length of cotton before attempting to thread the needle as the cotton may need to be trimmed several times before it is successfully

threaded. Leave the yarn on the reel, thread the needle and then cut off the required length. You might even thread several needles on to the reel before beginning work, taking each off in turn with a suitable length of thread.

Use a strong, fine cotton or polyester thread in a colour that matches the beads, and use it double if possible. Always fasten thread ends securely. Start with a knot and, if working on canvas, take the yarn around a thread of the fabric and stitch into the knot. Finish off each length of thread firmly with back stitching and work a French knot into the stitches to give them extra strength.

F L O R A L   F O O T S T O O L

This is one of a pair of Victorian beadwork footstools. Floral designs such as this were a favourite subject of the era, for every type of embroidery. A border of tent stitch in black wool has been added to make the embroidery fit the footstool and to make it easier to mount.

Size
The finished beadwork is 10in (25cm) in diameter.

MATERIALS

(The footstool is worked with round beads of about $\frac{1}{16}$in (1.5mm) diameter.)

Beads in your choice of colours
Strong sewing thread in neutral or colours to match the beads
Beading needles
12-mesh double-thread canvas
Beeswax (to wax the thread). If beeswax is not easily available, an ordinary domestic wax candle can also be used.

ORDER OF STITCHING

Fold the canvas in half each way to find the centre. Baste along the fold lines using coloured thread. Work the design following the chart. The centre is indicated by arrows. Start in the centre. You can work the areas of the design in any order, but it is easier to work a patterned area first and then fill in the background around it. Use thread doubled if possible and work in either beaded half cross stitch or beaded tent stitch throughout. (Refer to page 64 for the techniques.) Do not mix the stitches as they will pull against each other.

If you prefer, the background can be worked in Berlin woolwork to make the beadwork stand out in relief. If the beadwork is in beaded half cross stitch, use half cross stitch for the background. If you are using beaded tent stitch then use tent stitch for the wool work.

Detail of Floral Footstool.

G O T H I C   C U S H I O N

The beadwork on this cushion probably began as part of a valance designed to fit along a mantelpiece or over a window. A later hand has stitched two pieces of border on to a velvet background. The centre line and the edges have been finished with a thick cord in toning colours. The advantage of using this type of design is that you can suit the number of repeats to the size of the cushion you want to make.

The medieval influence is found in much Victorian art, as seen here in the Gothic Cushion.

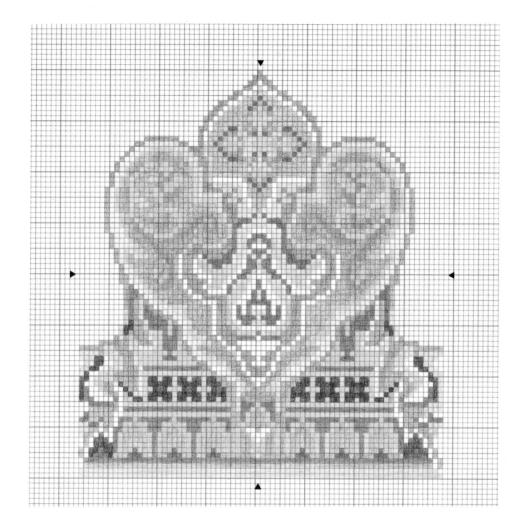

Left: Working chart for the beadwork motif. If you prefer, you can do the entire cushion front on canvas, working a background in woolwork first, then working the beadwork design afterwards. Use either half cross stitch or tent stitch for both embroidery and beadwork.

The design could also be used for a bag. Work two separate motifs, make them up into a bag, and finish with a cord stitched around the edges and along the top. For a special touch, you might attach a tassel to the bottom point.

Size
Approx 18 × 12 in (45 × 30cm)

MATERIALS

The cushion is worked in round beads of about $\frac{1}{16}$in (1.5mm) diameter.

Beads in your choice of colours

Strong sewing thread in neutral or colours to match the beads.
Beading needles
12-mesh double-thread canvas
Beeswax (to wax the thread)

ORDER OF STITCHING

Fold the canvas in each way to find the centre. Baste along the fold lines using coloured thread. Work the design following the chart on this page. Use thread double if the hole in the bead is large enough. Use either beaded half cross stitch or beaded tent stitch throughout (refer to page 64). It is important that all stitches slant in the same direction.

SILKEN BEADED PURSE

This small silk purse is worked with very small gold-coloured glass beads in a geometric repeat pattern. The back and front are the same, the design having been worked in one strip and then folded to make the bag. The embroiderer cleverly chose a fabric with a clear vertical line to guide the stitches. The design would look just as effective on a plain matt silk.

Size
4 × 3½in (10 × 9cm)

MATERIALS

Tiny round gold-coloured glass beads ¹⁄₂₅in (1mm) diameter – approximately 1,200
Pale turquoise fabric 9 ×4½ in (23 × 12cm)
Strong fine thread in the background colour
Fine beading needles
Beeswax or candle (to wax thread)

ORDER OF STITCHING

Trace the design and transfer it to the fabric. Stitch the beads in place with back stitch, using a single thread in the needle.

Above: detail of the beaded purse.
Opposite: Small, beaded purses, shaped like Dorothy bags on a drawstring, were simple to make and usually matched the gown. Beads or gold-thread embroidery were used to embellish evening purses for a special effect.

14

SAMPLERS

Samplers date back at least to the seventeenth century, when professional embroiderers made them as a record of their stitches and designs and on these early samplers the stitching is often exceptionally fine. Later, as they learned to sew, children made samplers to practise their stitches. These examples usually feature pictures of birds, people, trees, flowers and buildings, but out of proportion to each other and often two-dimensional with no attempt at perspective.

By the nineteenth century samplers had become more simple, and often only cross stitch was used. Neatness of work was all important.

Samplers were also used as a means of teaching other lessons besides needlework and neatness. For example, they might take the form of multiplication tables or, of course, the alphabet. Many are designed around a biblical text or feature some moral lesson. The Victorians were obsessed with death and it was not unusual for a child of six or eight years old to make a sampler with words anticipating her own mortality, or commemorating a dead sibling.

In schools for the poor and in orphanages, girls destined for domestic service would learn to do all sorts of plain sewing and would sometimes work a sampler. This would usually be closely covered with alphabet letters of different sizes and types and often had a variety of borders. The alphabets were invaluable for marking household linen, as noted in a contemporary manual for the National Female Schools of Ireland: 'Marking in cross stitch, though very much superseded by the use of marking ink, is yet sufficiently useful, and is still so generally practised as to render a knowledge of the proper mode of doing so an indispensable part of the business of a National School for teaching plain-work.' Today, samplers are worked for pleasure or as a decorative way to mark an important family occasion.

FABRICS

Cross stitch samplers are always worked on evenweave fabric which dictates the rather formal and stylized patterns produced. The examples in this chapter, one recently made and two from the nineteenth century, are worked on fabrics of different thread count. The fabrics usually chosen for samplers today are Aida (11, 14 or 18 threads to 1in (2.5cm)); Hardanger fabric (22 threads to 1in (2.5cm)); and Linda (27 threads to 1in (2.5cm)). These are all cotton fabrics and are available in white or off-white. (The latter darkens quite quickly to a soft creamy beige.) Some are available in colours such as pink and blue, which might be used for birth samplers, or in holly green which is lovely for Christmas themes. Linen, which looks beautiful and is pleasant to work on, is also available in a variety of thread counts, but is comparatively expensive.

STITCHES AND PATTERNS

The samplers pictured in this chapter are all worked in simple cross stitch. When working, keep the stitches even and to ensure that the top threads of crosses lie in the same direction. The method for working cross stitch is on page 66.

'House and Garden' is a modern sampler designed on traditional Victorian themes and motifs.

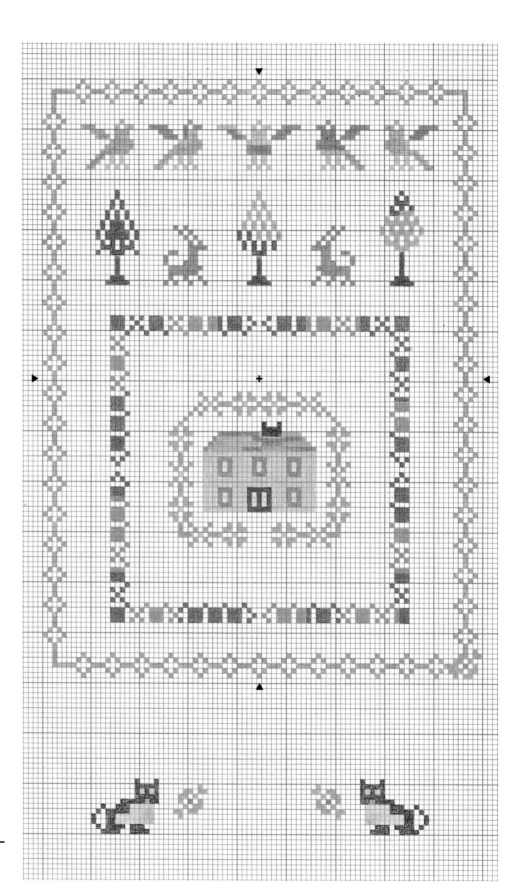

Today, samplers are worked for pleasure rather than as a task, as in the past. Traditional motifs, birds, deer, and the family cat are incorporated in this modern interpretation of a Victorian sampler.

H O U S E   A N D   G A R D E N
S A M P L E R

This is a modern sampler and represents a house surrounded by a flower garden, enclosed by a hedge. Outside is a forest, inhabited by deer and, above, a flock of birds fly in a blue sky. The deer and bird motifs are traditional and can sometimes be seen on old samplers.

Size

Sampler pictured measures 9 × 6¾in (23 × 17 cm).

MATERIALS

DMC stranded embroidery cotton, 1 skein each of the following colours:

- blue (809)
- shaded brown (105)
- yellow (743)
- shaded green (122)
- brown (801)
- light brown (841)
- shaded grey (53)
- shaded red (roof) (57)
- green (954)
- pink (963)
- lavender (210)
- blue (775)
- blue (792)

12 × 14in (30 × 35cm) of evenweave fabric, 27 threads to 1in (2.5cm)
Crewel embroidery needle
Embroidery frame

ORDER OF STITCHING

Following the chart and key, work the sampler in cross stitch. Use two strands of stranded cotton worked over two threads of the fabric for everything except the lettering, cats and tiny flowers. Work these in a single strand of cotton over one thread of fabric. A name can be worked centrally below the house, with the month and year above.

Detail from the House and Garden sampler.

A L P H A B E T
S A M P L E R

This sampler has been worked on 13-mesh double-thread white canvas with an embroidery thread closely resembling Coton à Broder. Cross stitches are worked over one double thread of the canvas.

The canvas seems to have been specially made for samplers as it has a red and blue border. The design would work just as well on evenweave fabric with the woven border replaced with one of the patterns from the sampler. You can work the sampler following the original, or you may prefer to select different elements to create your own design. For example, a verse from one of your favourite poems could be combined with a double border of the wave pattern.

Like many 19th-century samplers, this one is made up of a variety of different border patterns and the alphabet is in several different styles. The working chart is on the opposite page.

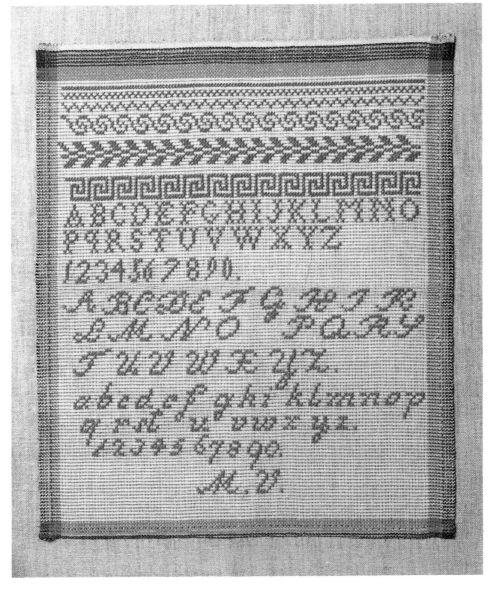

F L O W E R   A N D   B I R D
M O T I F S

This delightful sampler was worked in 1865 by Eliza Manser who was a pupil at Dover Charity School. It is worked on a very closely-woven fabric (about 38 threads to the inch), and the stitches are made over two threads.

The sampler features alphabets on different scales, border patterns and various motifs — crowns, a gardener, a bird, stylized flowers in a pot, a castle and a church. At the bottom there are three larger motifs, two of flowers and one of a bird and flowers. These motifs have been abstracted for you to work. The whole design is surrounded by a border of stylized rosebuds. The sampler is mainly in cross stitch, but one lower case alphabet is in back stitch worked over two threads to form squares.

The details are taken from the Dover Charity School Sampler (opposite). Above, *Posy of Flowers*, top right, *Bird amid Flowers*, right, *Rose*.
Charts for these designs are overleaf.

Elizabeth Manser's sampler was worked in 1865. As a pupil at a charity school she might well have been destined for domestic service and would have had to use her sewing skills to mark household linens.

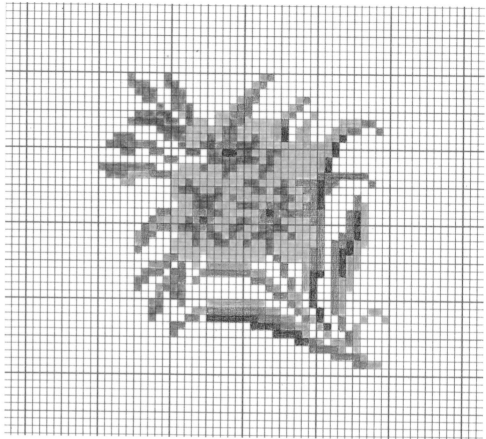

Detail from *Posy of Flowers* (see page 22). The chart (right) is indicated in colours that are keyed to the thread colours on the opposite page.

Detail from *Bird amid Flowers* (see page 22). The chart for working this design is on the right. Work the embroidery using the chart and the key to thread colours opposite. The chart for *Rose* is on the opposite page.

Size

This depends on the type of fabric chosen and the number of threads worked over.

MATERIALS

Evenweave fabric
DMC stranded embroidery cottons:

For the posy of flowers:

■ green (472)

■ green (3347)

■ green (367)

■ green (320)

■ green (368)

■ yellow (744)

■ brown (921)

■ rose pink (899)

For the bird amid flowers:

■ green (472)

■ green (3347)

■ green (367)

■ blue (813)

■ blue (825)

■ dark grey (413)

■ light grey (762)

■ beige (738)

■ light brown (436)

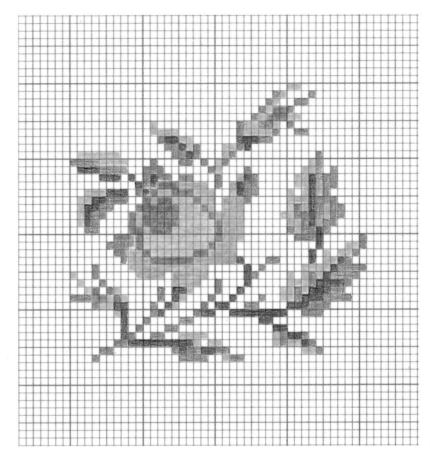

■ brown (434)

■ rose pink (899)

For the rose:

■ green (472)

■ green (367)

■ green (320)

■ rose pink (776)

■ rose pink (899)

Crewel embroidery needle

ORDER OF STITCHING

Work the designs following the charts and keys. Work in two strands of stranded embroidery cotton over two fabric threads throughout.

BERLIN
WOOLWORK

Berlin woolwork was the most popular kind of needlework in the second half of the nineteenth century. For centuries canvaswork had been practised with the patterns drawn out onto the canvas but in the early 1800s a German printer developed the idea of printing designs on to squared paper, which the embroiderer could copy. Each coloured square represented one stitch on the canvas. By the 1830s vast quantities of these patterns were being imported into England from Germany, together with the wools for working them, hence the name Berlin woolwork. Soon patterns were being designed and produced in both England and America, and were frequently given away with magazines.

So popular was Berlin woolwork that examples of it were to be found everywhere in the Victorian home. It was used for covering stools and chairs and as pictures, for bell pulls, tie-backs, valances, tablecloths and carpets.

Although samplers exist showing a wide variety of stitches for Berlin woolwork, most of the embroidery was carried out in tent stitch, cross stitch or half cross stitch.

Double and single thread canvases of different weights were used, including a very fine silk canvas which was attractive enough for the background to be left unworked.

All three designs given in this chapter are worked in either half cross stitch or tent stitch. Canvas is available in white, which is best for pale colours, or antique, which is best for mid or dark colours. The mesh of the canvas refers to the number of threads to 1in (2.5cm). For example, 12-mesh canvas has 12 threads and 11 holes to 1in (2.5cm). It is always best to work in a frame.

Hundreds of pairs of slippers must have been embroidered for husbands, fathers and uncles during Queen Victoria's reign and Berlin woolwork was the favourite medium.

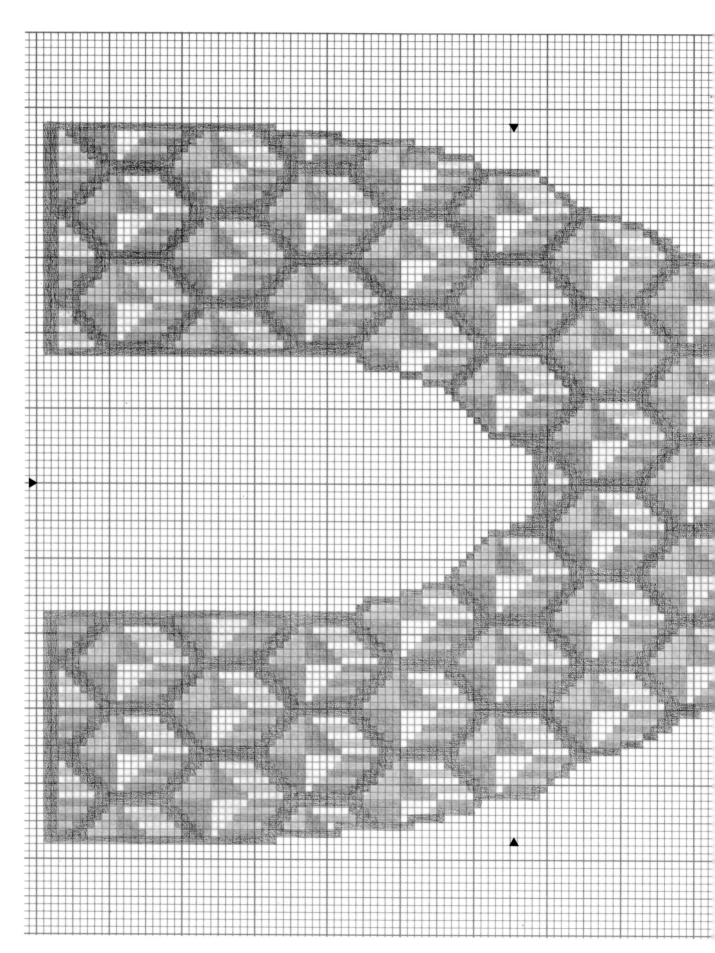

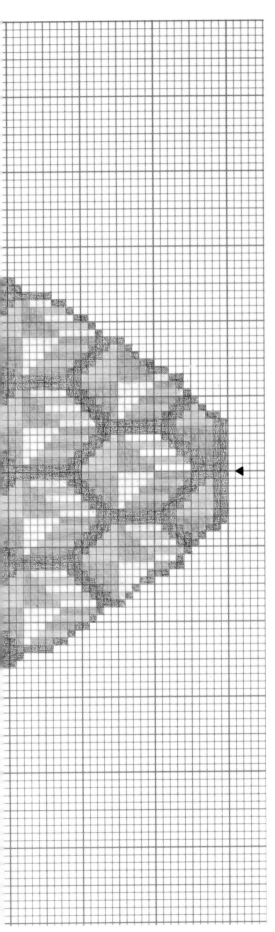

S L I P P E R S

Geometric repeat patterns like this one are particularly suitable for slippers as you simply draw out the slipper to size on the canvas. Then, starting at the centre front, repeat the pattern until you have covered the shape. The slippers have been lined with a thin felt and the edges finished with a cord. The soles are felt, but could equally well be of chamois leather.

Size

The pattern is for an English man's size 8 (US size 42).

MATERIALS

DMC tapestry wools:

- ■ black – 7 skeins

- □ light grey (7282) – 2 skeins

- □ pink (7759) – 2 skeins

- ■ burgundy (7139) – 2 skeins

11-mesh double thread canvas
Tapestry needle
Tapestry frame

ORDER OF STITCHING

Draw out the slipper shape to the correct size on the canvas. Following the chart and key, work the pattern all over the drawn shape. Start working at the centre front. Half cross stitch is probably better than tent stitch for this design as it produces a thinner and more pliable fabric for making up into slippers. Work a second slipper; finish the edges with a decorative cord.

The chart for the slippers is on the opposite page. A detail of the pattern is above.

CHRYSANTHEMUM CUSHION

This design was based on a pretty motif of oriental-style chrysanthemums found on some Victorian china. Following the chart and key, work the design in half cross stitch.

Size
13 × 13in (33 × 33cm)

MATERIALS

DMC tapestry wools:

☐ white – 7 skeins

▨ blue (7797) – 2 skeins

▪ dark blue (7796) – 2 skeins

▨ gold (7782) – 1 skein

▨ green (7382) – 1 skein

▨ light brown (7463) – 1 skein

▪ brown (7801) – 1 skein

▨ light peach/brown (7176) – 1 skein

▨ rust (7360) – 1 skein

▨ dark rust (7303) – 1 skein

▨ peach (7175) – 1 skein

11-mesh canvas in antique colour
Tapestry needle
Tapestry frame

The design and colouring of this cushion was taken from the pattern on a set of Victorian china by Ridgeways called Fantasia.

T U R K I S H - S T Y L E
C A S E

This case is worked in two shades of a very fine wool and two shades of twisted embroidery cotton. The contrast between the soft matt wool and the shiny twisted cotton gives textural interest. The pattern, reminiscent of Turkish carpets, which were a very popular Victorian theme, was adapted from a border design for a table cover, published in a magazine of the 1870s. The case is backed and the top edge is bound with red felt, but you may prefer to work both sides of the case to match.

The Turkish influence can be seen reflected in Victorian paintings, ceramics, carpets, furnishings and in embroidery. Stylized minarets form the design here.

Size

6½ × 3in (16.5 × 7.5cm)

MATERIALS

The following quantities are sufficient to work both sides of the spectacles case.

DMC Broder Médicis wool:

■ red (8127) – 4 skeins

■ pale tangerine (8129) – 2 skeins

DMC Coton Perlé:

■ turquoise (991) 1 skein

■ turquoise (993) – 1 skein

15-mesh single thread canvas
Tapestry needle
Tapestry frame

ORDER OF STITCHING

Following the chart and key, work the case front in tent stitch. (Tent stitch is better than half cross stitch as it fills in the canvas more successfully and gives the work more body.) Use three strands of the wool together. Use a single strand of the Coton Perlé. Work a second side in the same way.

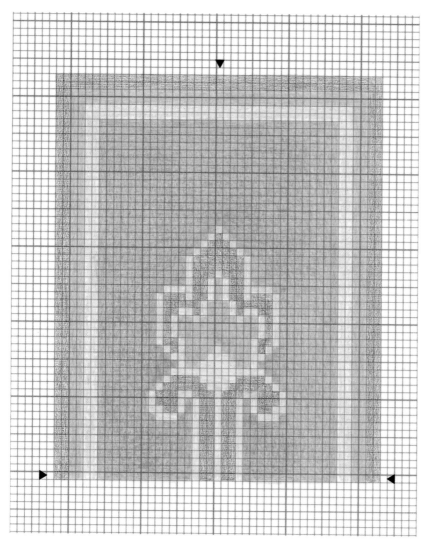

G O L D E N   B E E   B O X

Canvas lace was a fashionable technique for bordering pieces of Berlin woolwork, and numerous repeat patterns for it can be found on some Victorian samplers. *The Englishwoman's Domestic Magazine* offered a diagram sheet for 'The Chantilly Lambrequin for mantelpiece, what-not and bracket borders'.

The open lacy effect of the box is created by using cross stitch in a fine black thread on a white canvas. The lid of the box is worked in two different thicknesses of black thread and a fine gold machine embroidery thread. The bee in the centre is embroidered in gold and bronze beads. The design would work equally well as a picture. Alternatively, it could be enlarged to make a table centre,

make it into a clutch bag by extending the border to surround a row of bees.

Size
4¼ × 4¼in (10.06 × 10.06cm)

MATERIALS

Stranded embroidery cotton, black
– 1 skein (shown grey)
Appleton's crewel wool, black
– 1 skein (shown black)
Madeira machine embroidery thread no.40, gold (8) – 1 spool
18-mesh single thread white canvas
Round bronze and gold beads
Tapestry needle
Beading needle

ORDER OF STITCHING

Following the chart and key and using a single thread of black or gold yarn as appropriate, work the border design, centre panel and bee's wings in cross stitch over two threads of canvas. Fill in the scallops around the outer edge of the border with upright cross stitch worked with three strands of the gold yarn over two threads of canvas. Sew on the beads for the insect's body with one or two strands of black stranded cotton, using back stitch. For this you should ignore the threads of the canvas and stitch the beads where necessary to make a pleasing shape. (It is best to use back stitch to sew on these beads rather than beaded tent or half cross stitch, either of which would give too rigid and open an effect.) Finally, add the feelers in back stitch with a single strand of cotton.

Below and opposite:
In contrast to the strict geometry of the rest of the design, the bee's body is worked freehand, without regard for the threads of the canvas.

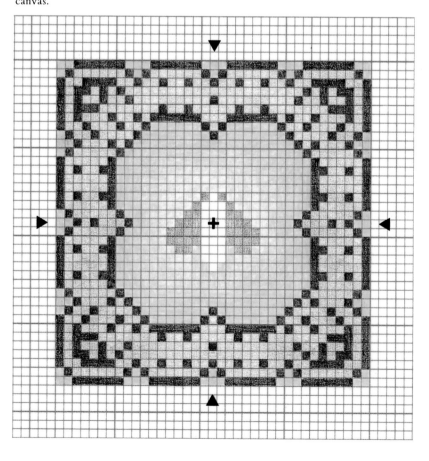

SURFACE
EMBROIDERY

Although Berlin woolwork was the most popular form of needlecraft from the 1860s onwards, ordinary surface embroidery did not lose its appeal. Many of the items that were decorated with Berlin woolwork were considered equally suitable for other forms of embroidery.

Flowers, both stylized and naturalistic, were the most frequently used motifs. Embroiderers could either draw up their own designs or they could use one of the numerous patterns offered by magazines. Even the latter gave scope for personal interpretation in the choice of threads, fabrics and colours. Fabrics used included silk, satin, velvet, sateen, cotton, felt and leather. Yarns ranged from stranded silk or cotton, twisted silk and wool to metal threads.

Opposite: Many Victorian women owned a soft, lightweight stole like this. It would have been worn for a little warmth with low-necked dresses.

The design of naturalistic flowers on this evening bag was taken directly from the left-hand panel of the valance (see picture left, page 40). The trace-off pattern is above, left. Follow the colours indicated on the pattern for threads.

ORDER OF STITCHING

Trace the design and transfer it to the fabric. Work the embroidery following the colours of the trace-off pattern. Use a single strand of thread unless otherwise stated. The leaves and forget-me-nots are worked in satin stitch. The buds are worked in long chain stitches. The red stems are in stem stitch as are the stems of the forget-me-nots to the left of the centre. All other stems are worked in split stitch using two strands of thread.

41

HANDKERCHIEF
FOR A LADY

Flowers are again the theme for this delicate handkerchief with its limited palette of pale colours. The bold, simple design is enhanced by the contrast between the heavy twisted yarn and the fine silk on which it is worked. The design is composed of a central garland made up of four repeats of two flowers and two sprays of leaves with a repeated corner motif. The colours have been varied for different flowers so that, for example, two of the large corner roses are pink while the other two are cream. The edge is scalloped and finished with buttonhole stitch.

This is a very adaptable design. It could be repeated to make a dressing table mat or it could be used for a tea tablecloth. For this, you could create a large central garland by increasing the number of repeats and using the corner motifs just as they are. Change the fabric and yarn to suit the purpose of the embroidery.

Size

13 × 13in (32.5 × 32.5cm)

MATERIALS

16in (40cm) – square of off-white fine silk fabric

DMC Coton Perlé no.8 thread, 1 skein each of the following colours:
shaded green (94)
cream (712)
pink (818)

Fine embroidery crewel needle

ORDER OF STITCHING

Buttonhole-stitch the edges of the fabric. Trace the design and transfer it to the fabric. Following the colours of the trace-off pattern, work the embroidery. The large roses are in satin stitch. Work each petal separately and change the direction of the stitches in each case to give an effect of light and shade. The other solid flowers, buds and leaves are also in satin stitch. Take the stitches across each petal or leaf, working along the length from end to end. The star-shaped flowers are worked in single straight stitches and all the stems are worked in long back stitches.

Time has faded the bright colours of the original embroidery on this handkerchief, but the design is still well-defined because of the contrast between the filmy fabric and the texture of the thread.

ALPHABET
FOR
LINENS

For purely utilitarian purposes, Victorian ladies marked household linens with Indian ink or, sometimes, with cross stitch letters. However, personal possessions were often marked in a much more decorative way with imposing initial letters or monograms.

A variety of different styles of alphabet was available to the embroiderer from quite simple scrolling letters to elaborate Gothic ones or imitation strapwork. Many were additionally decorated with flowers and might also be topped by a coronet. In the latter case, it was important not to get the style appropriate for a viscount mixed up with that intended for a baron!

Such 'useful' work as embellishing sheets, towels, pillowcases and so on with initials or monograms was considered appropriate for the lady of the house, and a young bride was expected to decorate the household linen for her trousseau in this way.

The alphabet on pages 46–47 is a quite straightforward one which can be used as single initials or for monograms. Work the letters in padded satin stitch over a very close filling of long running stitches to give a pronounced raised line.

This original piece of Victorian embroidery is typical of many pretty alphabets that even today can sometimes be found in 19th-century needlework books.

Cotton sheets, pillowcases etc on
which to work
Stranded embroidery cotton in the
same colour
Fine embroidery crewel needle
Embroidery frame

ORDER OF WORKING

Trace the appropriate letter or
letters and transfer to the fabric.

Positioning individual letters
–either a single initial or two or
three in a spaced row – presents
few problems. Remember that on
sheets, the initial or monogram
should be the right way up when
the sheet is turned back over the
blankets. (That is, wrong way up to
the person in the bed.)

When making a monogram of
linked, or overlapping initials, however, you will need to plan more
carefully.

The modern alphabet given
here is ideal for house linens
or clothing and could be
embellished with tiny
flowers and leaf tendrils for
a pretty look.

46

Trace each letter on to a separate piece of tracing paper and try different arrangements until you find one that pleases you. Then decide how the letters should interlace (ie., which lines go over which, and where sections should be removed altogether). With the monogram pictured on page 45, part of the final downstroke of the M has been omitted as has the final curl.

Make a tracing of the final arrangement and transfer it to the fabric.

Work the letters in padded satin stitch. Use four strands of stranded embroidery cotton for the filling and two strands for the satin stitch. Work sufficient long running stitches to fill the shape. You will need several rows of these filling stitches on the 'fat' areas of the letter and a single row for the 'thin' ones. Cover with very closely worked satin stitches.

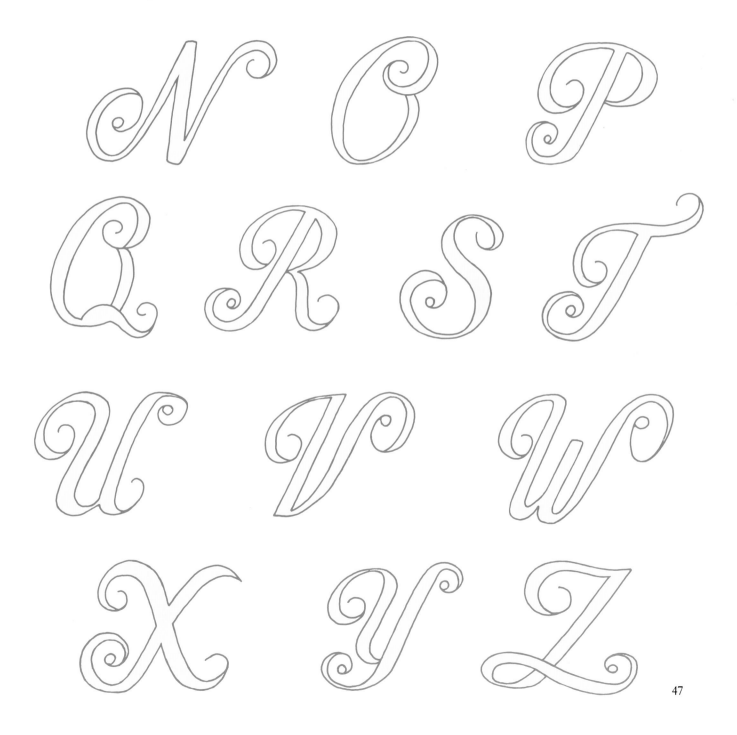

RIBBONWORK

Ribbons were used in a variety of different ways in Victorian embroidery. Sometimes they were woven in and out of a non-fraying fabric (such as canvas or leather) to make a bag or a case to hold small pieces of work. Very narrow ribbons were used instead of threads for canvaswork. Lustrous silk ribbons were used (sometimes with conventional threads) to create embroidered pictures.

Although modern polyester satin ribbons are not as soft and flexible as silk, they neither fade nor rot and are more likely to last than Victorian ribbon embroideries.

FLOWER PICTURE

Victorian ladies frequently incorporated narrow, silk, shaded ribbons into their embroidery. This gave their work an attractive three-dimensional effect and subtle changes of colour.

Ribbons were sometimes made up into flower shapes, such as rosebuds, and stitched in to the work. They were also used in the same way as conventional embroidery threads. Occasionally, ribbons were folded and caught down on the folds with tiny stitches. Stitches used with ribbons were simple-straight stitch, lazy daisy stitch, French knots and bullion knots.

Modern synthetic ribbons are not as easy to use as silk ribbons but they do come in a wonderful range of colours. Use them in conjunction with embroidery in stranded cotton or silk for the best results. The contrast between the raised areas of ribbon and the flatter thread stitches gives both depth and interest to a piece.

Choose strong fabric to work on, such as silk satin, taffeta, furnishing sateen or curtain lining. You need a fabric which will not be damaged by jerking the ribbon through it. Use a large-sized needle that will make a large hole and so avoid too much pulling.

Size
Design fits an oval 7 × 5in (18 × 13cm)

When this ribbon picture was made, the colours were the bright ones of fresh flowers. Now they have faded to the soft yellows and browns of dried ones.

MATERIALS

Cream fabric for the background
Offray polyester satin ribbons,
1⅛yd (1m) each of the following
colours:
buttercup yellow ⅛in (3mm) wide
yellow gold ¹/₁₆in (1.5mm) wide
willow ¹/₁₆in (1.5mm)-wide
DMC stranded embroidery cotton,
1 skein each of the following
colours:
yellow (727)
gold (743)
light green (3348)

Large-sized embroidery crewel
needle (for ribbon)
Fine embroidery crewel needle (for
stranded cotton)

ORDER OF WORKING

Trace the design and transfer it to
the fabric. (It is really only necessary to draw in the position of the
stems as a guide for the rest of the
embroidery.)

Work the thread embroidery
first. Use two strands of stranded
cotton throughout, except for the
small leaves near the top of the
stems where a single strand is used.
The stems are worked in stem
stitch and the leaves and some
flowers in lazy daisy stitch. Flower
centres, some complete flowers and
the 'lupins' at the top are worked
in French knots. The hanging flowers are worked in bullion knots.

Next, work the ribbon embroidery. The leaves and star-shaped
flower near the centre of the
bouquet, as well as the buds running up the stems are in straight
stitch. (The flower centre is a
French knot in stranded cotton.)

Make four flowers using the
buttercup-coloured ribbon and four
in the yellow gold ribbon in the
following way: cut a 2in (5cm)
length of ribbon, run a gathering
thread along the centre, pull up to
make a flower shape and stitch into
place on the picture.

Finally, make a double bow from
the two shades of yellow ribbon
and stitch in place to 'tie' the
bouquet (see picture on page 49).

Follow this trace-off for the
Flower Picture. Use ribbon to
complete the bouquet.

51

F L O R E N T I N E

This needlecase cover in ribbon canvaswork has been worked in a version of the Florentine pattern which has been a favourite for centuries and was so popular for Berlin woolwork.

The stitch is a straight stitch which has many names including Florentine stitch, flame stitch and Irish stitch.

The needlecase is worked in the narrowest available double-faced ribbon – $\frac{1}{16}$in (1.5mm) wide on 13 threads to 1in (2.5cm) single thread canvas. This mesh enables the ribbons to lie flat and still cover the canvas adequately. Alternatively, $\frac{1}{8}$in (3mm)-wide ribbons and 11-thread canvas could be used. Choose white canvas for pale ribbons and 'antique' colour for dark shades.

It is essential to keep the ribbons flat, at least on the right side of the work. Using double-faced satin ribbon ensures that even if it twists on the back of the work it will still look right side up on the front.

Choose closely-related shades of the same colour for a subtle effect.

For more drama, select colours from the same family but widen the difference between the shades and add a contrasting accent. Here, three orangey shades – rust, orange and peach – are accented with a rich green.

Size
3¾ × 3¼in (9.5 × 8cm)

MATERIALS

13-mesh single thread canvas (large enough piece to be held in an embroidery frame)
$\frac{1}{16}$in –wide (1.5mm) Offray double-faced satin ribbon in the following colours and amounts:

forest green – 9yds (8m)

rust – 5yds (4.5m)

peach – 5yds (4.4m)

torrid orange – 3⅞yds (3.5m)

Tapestry needle
Embroidery frame

ORDER OF WORKING

Following the chart and key, work the book cover in Florentine stitch. Work the first row alternating the length of the stitches – the first stitch over four threads, the second over three, the third over four and so on. Work subsequent rows over four threads throughout until you reach the spine of the book where the pattern is three-four-three threads over the design.

The work is finished off with a row of stitches over three - four - three threads as at the beginning.

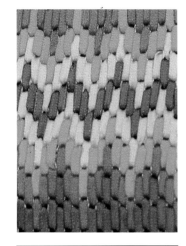

Above: Detail of the Florentine needlecase in ribbon work.
Below: Working chart for the Florentine pattern.

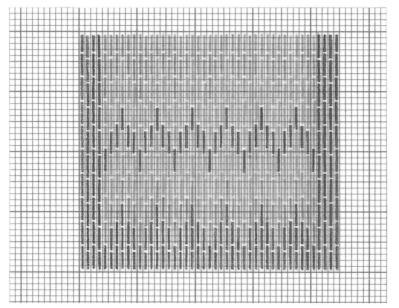

CREWELWORK

Towards the end of the nineteenth century there was a revival of interest in historical types of embroideries, particularly the crewelwork of the seventeenth century. This type of embroidery, often called Jacobean work, was originally worked in wool on a linen/cotton twill fabric. Designs owed a great deal to those found on imported Indian textiles but they also incorporated the flora and fauna of the English countryside. A central theme was the Tree of Life, laden with scrolling leaves and exotic fruit. Colourful tropical birds might fly through the branching stems and the foreground was usually composed of plants in a hummocky landscape. This would be populated with a huntsman and a variety of animals – usually all much of a size.

Stitches were usually simple ones such as stem stitch, long-and-short stitch, satin stitch, buttonhole stitch and chain stitch. Fillings included French knots, squared filling and honeycomb filling.

Nineteenth-century work followed the same themes as the earlier pieces. Crewel wools on linen or crash (a coarser linen) were the favourite materials for making window and door curtains. The latter, called *portières*, were fashionable in artistic circles – and they were also an excellent way of avoiding draughts!

This *portière*, worked in crewel wools on a beige wool twill, has all the traditional design elements. The Tree of Life grows from a landscape in which a huntsman pursues a quarry as big as himself over a hilly, flowery landscape. The leafy tree bears different sorts of blossom, including thistles and a mixture of fruit. Pomegranates exist side by side with acorns with a delightful disregard for seasonal and geographical realism. The cushion is based on just two elements of the curtain.

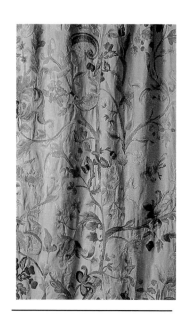

Detail of the door curtain (opposite). American crewelwork has a characteristic style and excellence of execution comparable to anything produced in Europe.

54

POMEGRANATE
AND PARROT

The fabric used here is a closely-woven cotton furnishing sateen but linen or linen-look fabric, or satinized cotton (sold especially for surface embroidery), or even curtain lining could be used.

Size

16 × 16in (40 × 40cm)

MATERIALS

Cream or beige fabric 19 × 19in (48.5 × 48.5cm)
Appleton crewel wool, 1 skein each of the following colours:
gold (475, 695)
old gold (313)
beige (984, 985)
khaki (954)
brown (955, 904)
pale blue (152)
blue-green (643, 645, 646)
yellow-green (251A, 253, 254)
maroon (147)
pink (121, 142, 143)

Medium-sized crewel needle
Embroidery frame

ORDER OF STITCHING

Trace the design on pages 58–59 and transfer it to the fabric. Work the embroidery following the colours of the trace-off pattern. It does not really matter in which order you do this but it is probably easier to work the solid parts of the pattern before the areas of open filling. Use one strand of wool throughout.

Most areas are worked with long and short stitch. This includes the small flower and its leaf, the leaves and 'petals' of the pomegranate, the bird's head and some areas of its wings and tail. The bird's legs and body are in stem stitch, with the body in parallel lines curving around the shape. The long tail feather is in stem stitch and satin stitch and the smallest tail feather, individual wing feathers and beak are also in satin stitch. The pupil of the bird's eye is a French knot.

The thick stem (part of the 'tree') is made up of lines of stem stitch and the centre of the small leaf is a single line of the same stitch. The stem of the small flower and the central veins of the pomegranate leaves are in satin stitch. French knots make the centre of the small flower and outline the central section of the pomegranate. This section is filled with individual cross stitches. The outer section is filled with squared filling stitch.

Lay the lines of the trellis first, then hold in place by small stitches.

Detail of the Pomegranate and Parrot cushion (opposite). Geometric patterning with stylized plants and foliage and exotic animals and birds was a feature of crewelwork designs from the 17th century onwards.

Trace-off patterns for the
cushion on page 57.
The colours used on the
trace-off are keyed to the
crewelwork wools listed
on page 56.

PINCUSHIONS

In Victorian times, pincushions were not just practical accessories for holding pins and needles, they were highly decorative objects made as Valentines and to commemorate births and weddings. A very popular form was a small, tightly-stuffed cushion on which a pattern was formed in pins or in beads speared on pins. There would be a name and possibly a sentimental message and appropriate motifs such as hearts, flowers and leaves. Additional decoration might be of lace and ribbon. The cushions would rarely have been used, since removing pins would have spoilt the pattern (as would sticking in more pins).

These little cushions are easy to make and most therapeutic to work.

MAKING PINCUSHIONS

Fillings: You need a firm base to work on and to hold the pins securely. Bran and sawdust are a good choice, but they must be thoroughly dry before you use them. Emery powder and iron filings were frequently used in the past on the basis that they would keep the pins sharp. In fact, these fillings are inclined to rust the pins. You could also choose a soft filling such as natural animal wool or used knitting wool. Synthetic fillings are also a possibility, although it can be difficult to pack them into the cushion tightly enough.

FABRICS

Always make an undercover of a closely-woven fabric such as calico or plain white cotton to hold the filling.

Top covers can be of almost anything you like. Velvet is pleasant and easy to work on,

and it has the advantage that, if you change your mind about the placing of a pin, the mark will not show (provided you remove the pin quickly). It is also a practical choice if you want to be able to use the cushion.

Pale-coloured silk or satin are lovely for layette or wedding pincushions. However, pin marks will show on these fabrics so you cannot change your mind halfway through a design.

You might like to use a lacy fabric over a coloured one, picking out part of the lace design in beads.

SHAPES

Pincushions can be round, square, rectangular – or what you will but, in general, the simple shapes are best. If you want a particularly smooth covering, the boxed cushion shape works well. Whatever shape you choose, make sure it is deep enough to take the length of the pins.

PINS AND BEADS

Choose good-quality, fine dressmaking pins in a standard length. For delicate fabrics use fine 'wedding and lace pins'.

The beads used on all the cushions shown here are readily available in craft and needle-work shops. They are mostly small and inexpensive and are sold in a wide range of colours. The beads are threaded in ones or twos on to a pin and then the pin is stabbed straight into the cushion.

These velvet cushions are intended to be used as 'working' pincushions and the designs are, therefore, simple.
The silk cushions are intended as gifts and are more elaborate and delicate in execution.

A COLLECTION OF PINCUSHIONS

LILY-OF-THE-VALLEY CUSHION

Size

3 × 1¾in (7.5 × 4.5cm)
MATERIALS (for decoration)
Fine dressmaking pins
Small beads in gold, pink and green
Flower motif in lace
Beads of different sizes (to complement the type of lace flower)
Narrow lace edging

ORDER OF WORKING

The design on this small cushion is a simple one. Cover the seam round the edge with lace held in place by a row of beaded pins. Decorate the top with a lace flower motif. On the cushion shown here a whole lily-of-the-valley motif was used, plus the leaves cut from a similar motif.

Hold the flower area of the motif in place with beads of appropriate sizes and colour. Here, white beads graduate in size from the largest to the smallest blooms. Highlight the leaves with little green beads. Decorate the area between the lace edging and the flowers with a simple trellis pattern of beads.

LOVE BIRD CUSHION

The design on this larger velvet cushion was dictated by the lovebird lace motif on the top. What makes this piece particularly attractive is that the wings are left free, giving a three-dimensional effect.

The second important element was the choice of a furnishing braid to cover the edges. The braid gives the cushion a tailored look and gives scope for some large glittery beads which follow the scallops of the braid.

Size

3¼ × 3¼in (8 × 8cm)
MATERIALS (for decoration)
Fine dressmaking pins
Small beads in pink, gold, green and blue
Faceted glittery beads with one flat side
Lace motif
Furnishing braid, ½in (1cm)-wide

ORDER OF WORKING

Attach the braid around the edge of the cushion with glittery beads. The beads should follow the design, in this case a corded line making a double scallop. Position the bird motif and attach with pins to highlight the shapes. This motif shows a pair of lovebirds, so one has been highlighted with pink beads and the other with blue. Use a gold bead and a faceted bead for each. Highlight the leaves with green beads.

CHRISTENING CUSHION

This white silk-covered cushion is edged with palest pink lace and decorated largely with small pink pearl beads. The lace is wide with scallops on one side and zigzags on the other, and this has been made into a feature of the cushion. The lace is put on flat and is caught on the inner and outer angles of the

Using motifs of lace is a simple way of decorating a pincushion and a wide variety of motifs is available for every kind of scheme. Secure motifs with beads in relevant colours.

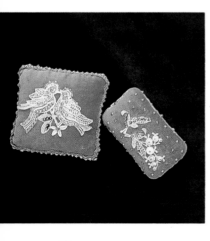

zigzag. To turn the corner, three points have been caught together.

Size

4½ × 4½in (11 × 11cm)
MATERIALS (for decoration)
Lace pins
Small pastel coloured pearl beads
Large, cup-shaped parly sequins
Wide lace trimming in the same colour
Silver pencil (or tracing paper and pencil)

ORDER OF WORKING

Attach the lace to the edge of the cushion, spacing the beads evenly around the edge of the lace.

Write the name of the child on the silk with the silver pencil and outline with beads. Alternatively, write the name in pencil on tissue paper and put in a pin on a bead at the beginning and end of the name to hold the paper in place. Then fill in the rest of the outline with beads and finally tear away the paper.

Finish off the design with bead and sequin flowers.

WEDDING CUSHION

This quite small cushion is made special by a large heart motif totally made up of pearl beads, and by the use of lace and ribbon.

Size

4 × 4in (10 × 10cm)
MATERIALS for decoration)

Lace pins
Pearl beads, ⅙in (4mm) diameter
Pearl beads, ⅛in (3mm) diameter
Ready-frilled non-fray lace
Offray blue feather-edge ribbon, ½in (1cm) wide
Silver pencil

ORDER OF WORKING

Fix the lace around the edge of the cushion with a few undecorated pins. Begin and end at the centre of the bottom edge, curving the ends of the lace with scissors.

Using ⅛in (3mm) beads, pin the ribbon in place to cover the bound edge of the lace. Start and finish the ribbon at the centre of the lace pleat. Fold a separate length of ribbon into a bow and fix it in place over the join with a pin and a ⅙in (4mm) bead.

Draw a simple heart shape centrally on the cushion top. Outline and fill with ⅙in (4mm) beads.

A christening pincushion is a novel and attractive way of commemorating a birth. You might incorporate the child's initials in the design. Similarly, they can be given as wedding or anniversary gifts.

STITCH LIBRARY

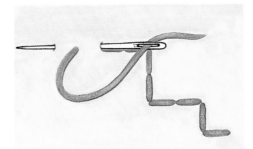

Back stitch This simple and useful stitch is used for outlining and, worked on a small scale, can follow quite intricate shapes accurately. Keep stitches even in size.

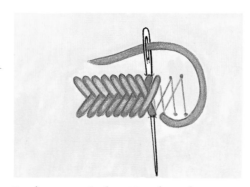

Basket stitch Work between marked parallel lines. This stitch is used either as a border or as a filling stitch.

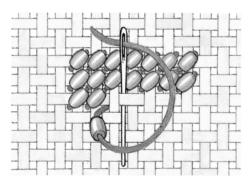

Beaded half cross stitch This is the simplest way to attach beads to canvas. Thread a bead on to each diagonal stitch, making sure that all the beads lie in the same direction.

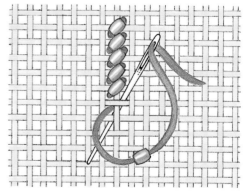

Beaded tent stitch Thread a bead on to the stitches as you work. Work vertically down the canvas. It is important that the bead size matches the canvas gauge. If beads are too large for the holes they will force the threads out of alignment and the beads will not lie neatly.

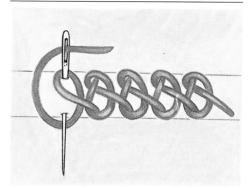

Braid stitch The band of stitching can be straight or curved. Keep the two sides of the braid parallel, and the stitches evenly neat.

Bullion knot This is worked in a similar way to a long French knot. ·Bring the needle up through the fabric, make a backstitch the intended length of the knot. wind the thread round the needle to make the desired length of knot.

Hold the thumb on the coiled thread, pull the needle through and re-insert it where it originally went into the fabric.

Buttonhole edging First, small running stitches are worked round the shape to hold the edge, then buttonhole stitch is worked to cover the running stitches.

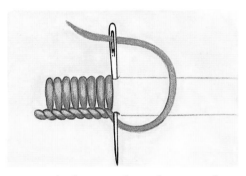

Buttonhole stitch This stitch is used extensively in cutwork and to give raw edges an attractive finish. It can be worked along curved and straight lines.

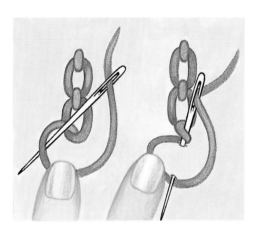

Cable chain stitch This outline stitch is similar to ordinary chain stitch but has a straight bar between each 'link' of the chain.

Chain stitch This stitch is used both for outlining and for filling a shape. The 'links' of the chain can be open and round or pulled tighter so that the 'link' chain closes.

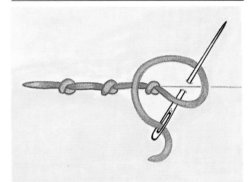

Coral stitch This outline stitch makes an attractive knotted line. Hold the thread loosely with the thumb while making the knot.

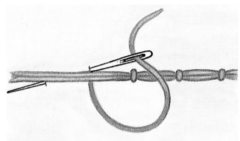

Couching This is a method of holding a thick thread, or several threads, down on the fabric surface, thus creating a raised line. Lay the thread to be couched along the design line and hold in place with the left (or non-working) hand. Tie down with a finer thread as shown. More stitches will be needed when working round a curve.

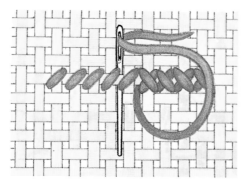

Cross stitch Modern samplers are usually worked in this stitch. It is particularly suited to evenweave fabrics. Cross stitch is worked in two stages, from right to left or left to right but the top stitch always lies in the same direction.

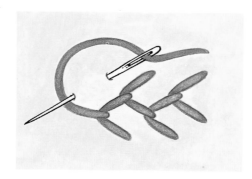

Feather stitch This stitch can be worked in straight lines or can follow a curve. In its simplest form, take one stitch to the right of the line, the next to the left and so on. Make multiple rows by working two or three stitches alternately on each side of the line.

Florentine stitch This is an upright stitch usually worked over four threads, staggering stitches so that the rows form zigzag lines. The pattern is made by using several colours.

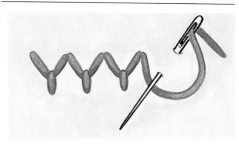

Fly stitch This stitch is worked singly in vertical or horizontal rows. Different effects can be achieved by varying the size, or the thickness of thread.

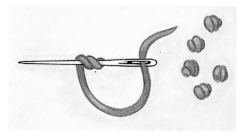

French knots This stitch is sometimes used for flower centres and can be used as a filling stitch. To work, take a small stitch and, with the needle still in the fabric, wind the thread twice round the needle. Hold the coiled thread in place as the needle is pulled through. Tighten the knot and re-insert the needle into the fabric where it first emerged.

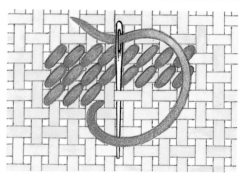

Half cross stitch This stitch looks like tent stitch when worked but uses less yarn and does not cover the canvas as well.

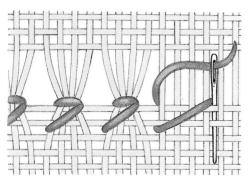

Hemstitch This is a decorative way of finishing the edges of items such as household linen and hand-kerchiefs. It can be worked on white linen, cotton or on delicate fabrics. Decide on the depth of hem needed plus turnings and withdraw two or three threads at this level. (To do this, snip threads in the cen-tre of the work and withdraw the threads each side. Darn in the ends of the drawn threads and cut off the excess.) Turn up the hem to the level of the withdrawn threads and baste in place. Work hemstitches as shown.

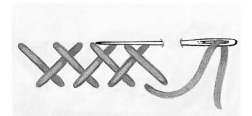

Herringbone stitch This is a border stitch and can be used as the basis for a variety of composite stitches. For the best effect, keep the spaces between the stitches even.

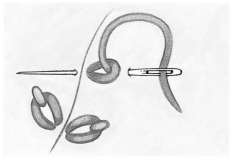

Lazy daisy (detached chain) stitch Work as for Chain stitch but hold each loop in place with a small stitch.

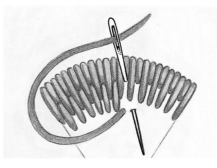

Long-and-short stitch This stitch is often used for shading. It is worked like satin stitch but the first row of stitches, outlining the shape, is worked with alternating long and short stitches. Subsequently, the stitches are all the same length.

Padded satin stitch (see also page 125) A slightly raised effect is created by first filling the shape with running, chain or stem stitches.

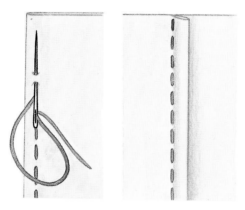

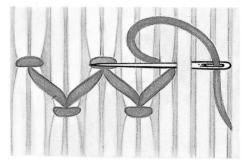

Chevron stitch Basically the same as surface honeycomb stitch but more widely spaced. The fabric is held very loosely.

Pintucks These tiny, decorative pleats are often worked on baby clothes and lingerie. Pleats can be as narrow as you like but never wider than 3mm (⅛in). Mark the top and bottom of the pleat's fold line, fold the fabric along this line and press. Measure and mark the required width of pleat and work a line of running stitches through both layers of fabric.

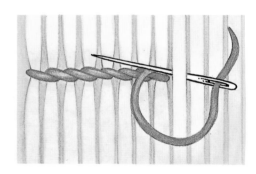

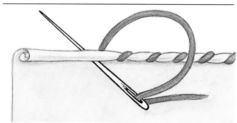

Rolled hem This is a pretty way to neaten the edge of a delicate fabric. Roll the edge gently between thumb and forefinger and, as you roll, stitch as shown.

Stem stitch This stitch is very like the stem stitch used in embroidery. It is the tightest of the stitches used in smocking and several rows are often worked at the top edge of a piece of work to 'set' the pleats.

SMOCKING STITCHES

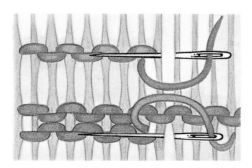

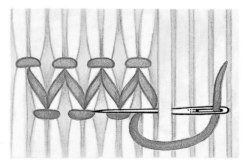

Cable stitch Not as tight a stitch as stem stitch it holds the gathers fairly firmly.

Surface honeycomb This is a loose stitch and is therefore usually worked at the bottom of a piece of smocking where fullness is needed.

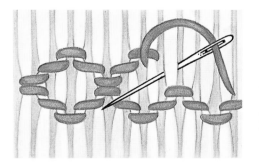

Wave stitch Rows of wave stitch can be worked with the preats aligned one below the other. Alternatively, make a diamond pattern by placing the 'crests' of one row immediately below the 'troughs' of the row above.

Satin stitch This is a useful stitch for filling shapes. When working, it is important that the shape is followed accurately to give it definition and that stitches are even and close together, completely covering the fabric. An effect of light and shade can be achieved by varying the direction of the stitch.

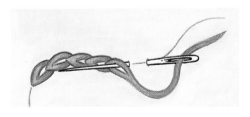

Split stitch This can be used for working stems, to outline, or it can be used as a filling. Soft twisted or floss (untwisted) thread works best for this stitch. The needle goes

through the thread, thus splitting it. Stranded thread can also be used and in this case, the needle passes between the strands.

Tent stitch This stitch can be worked in a diagonal direction or horizontally over the canvas.

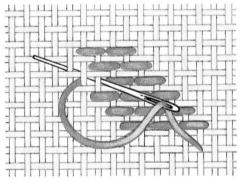

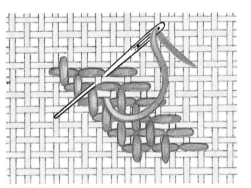

Upright cross stitch This is cross stitch worked with vertical and horizontal stitches (instead of diagonal stitches). It can be used as a filling stitch and contrasts effectively with conventional cross stitch.

LOG CABIN

Opposite: This silk coverlet was made in the 1880s by Mary Hannah Mitchelson and her sister Margaret Elizabeth – two prolific Cumbrian needle-women. It is made of 5in (12.5cm) squares, each consisting of 5 strips. The coverlet is particularly effective because one side of each square is black, which creates dramatic crosses against a brightly coloured background. The lace edging is particularly Victorian in style

Many people think that Log Cabin is a North American style of patchwork but it has a long tradition on both sides of the Atlantic. One of the oldest known types of patchwork, it was being done in Scotland by at least the middle of the eighteenth century and was popular in Ireland and England in the Victorian era.

The design has been known under a number of different names, including Roof Pattern, Canadian Logwood, Straight Patchwork and even the Mummy Pattern because a nineteenth-century writer thought it looked like the 'swathing bands of mummies'. The most widely-known name, however, is Log Cabin and it is made in a rather different way from most patchwork as the strips which go to make up the pattern are sewn to a foundation fabric, instead of the pieces being joined directly to one another. No template is needed as strips of fabric are made up into a square around a small central square.

The most common colour for the central patch was red with strips of light-coloured fabrics on two adjacent sides and dark colours on the other two sides. This is normally taken to represent the red glow of a fire casting light on one side of a room and causing shadows on the other.

Different fabrics were used for Log Cabin – woollens, silks, satin, velvets, or a mixture of fabrics. Because the patchwork is made by sewing on to a firmly-woven foundation fabric, it is quite possible to mix types and weights of fabric in the same piece of work.

The Victorians often used ribbons so the patchwork was sometimes known as Ribbon patchwork and the central square was quite likely to be embroidered.

When a number of Log Cabin squares have been made they can be arranged in a variety of different

ways. A popular Victorian arrangement can be seen in the antique Cumbrian quilt on page 71 and on the one below. Here the squares have been assembled in fours with all the light sides together. This means that when the quilt is made up, four dark sides are also together, making a pattern of light crosses on a dark ground and vice versa.

Another common design is that used for the Doll's ribbon quilt on page 76. For this the squares are assembled with the dark corners to one side. This design is known in America as Straight Furrows. An alternative version of the same pattern has been used for the Scrap bag Coverlet (see page 74)

by arranging the squares in the same way but changing the size of the squares. A double row of 8in (20cm) squares surrounds a central group of nine 16in (40cm) squares, each of which has a 4in (10cm) Log Cabin square in the centre.

There are numerous other possible arrangements as well as slightly different versions of the basic square. Courthouse (or Capital) Steps is such a design. Here, instead of two adjacent sides of the square being the same colouring, opposite sides are the same. A more complicated version, Pineapple, involves strips across the corners of squares as well as horizontal and vertical ones.

This Log Cabin patchwork coverlet was also made by the Mitchelson sisters and is in warm, woollen fabrics – probably intended as a carriage rug. Although the design is basically the same as the coverlet on page 13, this rug has a different feel about it, not only because of the choice of fabric but also because of the colouring, the number of strips making up a square, and the relatively large size of the central red patch

Opposite: With its rich colours and abundance of drapery, the Victorian parlour had a warm cosy feel.

SCRAP BAG COVERLET

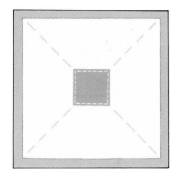

Pin and baste the central square centrally, right side up, on the foundation square

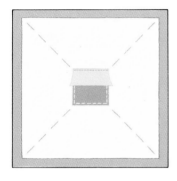

Pin and stitch a paler strip to the square, ¼in (6mm) from the edge

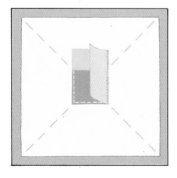

Pin and stitch a second strip along the second side of the square and then over the first strip

Victorian women frequently collected scraps of fabric, off-cuts from dressmaking, or good pieces cut from worn-out clothing or remnants. This coverlet is in this tradition, being made largely of manufacturer's samples.

Size

88in (2.2m) square (including borders) The quilt is made up from 64 8in (20cm) squares, 9 16in (40cm) squares and 9 4in (10cm) squares of Log Cabin. Each 16in (40cm) square is created round a 4in (10cm) one. The quilt is bordered with three strips of fabric, 1¼in (31mm), ¾in (18mm) and 2in (5cm) wide.

The method for making up a square of Log Cabin of whatever size is basically the same. The only variations are in the size of the central square and the width and number of the surrounding strips. Log Cabin patchwork can be made up either by hand or by machine. The strips are sewn into place and then the excess is cut off, so the length of the strips is immaterial. The instructions given here are for one 8in (20cm) square.

MATERIALS

White or natural coloured cotton foundation fabric (an old bed sheet is ideal).
Fabric in eight colours – four dark shades, four light ones – pieces at least 9×4in (23×10cm) for the strips.
Small piece of fabric for the central square (buy enough fabric for the centres of all the squares you need to make one article).
Sewing thread.
Seam allowance ¼in (6mm)

ORDER OF WORK

Cut all the fabric on the straight grain. Cut an 8½in (21.5cm) square of foundation fabric. Fold on the diagonals and press to mark the centre (or mark with lines of basting). This will help you to keep a good square when making up the Log Cabin.
Cut the four dark and four light fabrics into 1¼in (31mm) wide strips. Cut a 2¼in (5.7cm) square from the small piece of fabric.
Using the diagonal lines as a guide, pin and baste the square right side up,

centrally on to the foundation square (Fig 1).

Pin and then stitch a light coloured strip to the square, ¼in (6mm) from the edge with right sides together. Cut off the excess fabric (Fig 2). Turn back the strip and press. Pin and stitch a second strip of the same colour along the second side of the square and one short end of the first strip (Fig 3).

Repeat the process on the third and fourth sides of the square, using one of the dark fabrics. Continue with the other six fabrics in the same way, keeping the pale fabrics on one side of

the square and the dark ones on the other.

When the required number of Log Cabin squares have been made up sew them together in strips. Then sew the strips together.

NOTE As you will see from the antique quilts and this modern one, it is not essential for each square to be made from the same selection of fabrics. In fact, this is rarely seen with old examples. What is important is to make the centre of each square from the same fabric as this gives unity to the whole piece of work.

A modern coverlet made in the true patchwork tradition of using rag bag scraps with a variety of floral patterns in shades of maroon and inky blues. The scheme is unified by having all the central squares cut from one fabric and having a triple border. The squares have been arranged in a simple Straight Furrows design

DOLL'S RIBBON QUILT

This miniature bedcover is made from ribbon instead of fabric strips and the technique is slightly different. As there are no raw edges to enclose, the ribbon is top-stitched into place. The centre of each square is the traditional red, with creams and pinks on one side (the light colours) and three shades of blue, from pale to deep turquoise (the dark colours) on the other. In each case the palest of the three colours is placed closest to the centre.

Size
Approximately 11½×15in (29×38cm)

MATERIALS

2¼yds (2.5m) of 1in (2.5cm)-wide red ribbon
1¾yds (1.5m) each of ⅝in (15mm)-wide light cream and pale blue ribbons
2¼yds (2m) each of ⅝in (15mm)-wide cream and mid-turquoise ribbons
3yds (2.5m) each of ⅝in (15mm)-wide pink and deep turquoise ribbons
14×17in (35.5×43cm) piece of cotton foundation fabric
Sewing threads to match ribbons

ORDER OF WORK

The seam allowance on the ribbon strips is ⅛in (3mm) along the selvedge edges. Allow at least ¼in (6mm) on the cut edges as they will fray.
Cut 12 3¾in (9.5cm) squares of foundation fabric, on the straight grain. Mark the diagonals as described for Scrap bag coverlet (page 74).
Cut a piece of red ribbon 1½in (37mm) long (i.e. slightly longer than the width). Pin and baste it to the centre of the foundation square.
Place the cream ribbon, right side up, so that it overlaps one neatened edge of the red ribbon by ⅛in (3mm).

Pin and top-stitch in place with matching thread, making sure the stitches go through both ribbons. Cut off the excess cream ribbon.
Using the same colour and with right side up, pin and top-stitch the next piece of ribbon in place along the second side, overlapping the red ribbon to a greater degree to account for the extra width (i.e. you should finish with a central square). Repeat with the third and fourth sides using the pale blue ribbon.
Continue working around the square with the remaining four colours, using the darkest shades in each group on the outside.
Make up 11 more squares in the same way.
With right sides together, sew the squares together in four strips of three, working ⅛in (3mm) from the edge and with the blue ribbons to the left. Press lightly.
Join the strips together in the same way. Press lightly.
Top-stitch a strip of red ribbon along each short end of the cover. Then top-stitch another strip along each side.
The cover can be lined to make a coverlet or given an interlining as well to make a quilt.

Opposite: Ribbons have been used for this doll-sized bed cover. The design, popular in the nineteenth century, is called Straight Furrows

Left: Make up 12 squares to this colour scheme, using ribbons in 7 different colours

SQUARES
AND TRIANGLES

Simple squares and triangles can be arranged in numerous ways to make up a square block for a repeat design. This technique was particularly popular with settlers in the New World. Due to limited space it was simpler to make things that could be done in the lap and it was also possible for a number of people to piece blocks for the same quilt. It was only the making up into a complete top and, more particularly, quilting it, which needed more space. Homesteads were widely scattered and the task of quilting would often be the excuse for a quilting bee, a day-long get-together.

Block patterns are numerous and sometimes very complex and usually have very evocative names. This one is very effective in its freshness and simplicity, but so far as I can find out, has no name. The block is made up of four squares, turned through 45 degrees and framed with triangles to make another square. This square is then turned again with four more triangles used to make the complete square block.

Although patchwork and quilting are usually thought of as feminine occupations, there is a strong tradition of men being involved in both. Samuel Ross was such a man. He was born in the Canadian province of New Brunswick, but became apprenticed to a tailor in Boston, where he gained his sewing skills. He made this quilt with his wife, Matilda Ingram Ross, in the early years of this century. It was sewn by hand from work-shirt and pyjama fabrics, including some early homespun.

The quilt is made up of 36 12in (30cm) squares in checks and stripes. The fabrics vary from block to block, with mostly blues being chosen, plus some reds. The 5in (12.5cm) border is a small-print cotton. The finished patchwork was quilted in two designs. All of it, except the border which has chevrons worked over it, is quilted in a fan pattern.

Opposite: This quilt was made by a husband and wife team, Samuel and Matilda Ross, in the early part of the twentieth century. It was hand-pieced without papers, given a thin interlining and a cotton backing and then quilted

ONE-BLOCK CUSHION

This pattern is interesting enough to be used as a single block on a cushion, workbag or on the top of a stool. Five different checked and striped fabrics have been chosen for the block, with two of them also being used to border the design to create a cushion.

Make up this design using the American method, by hand or with a sewing machine (see page 110).

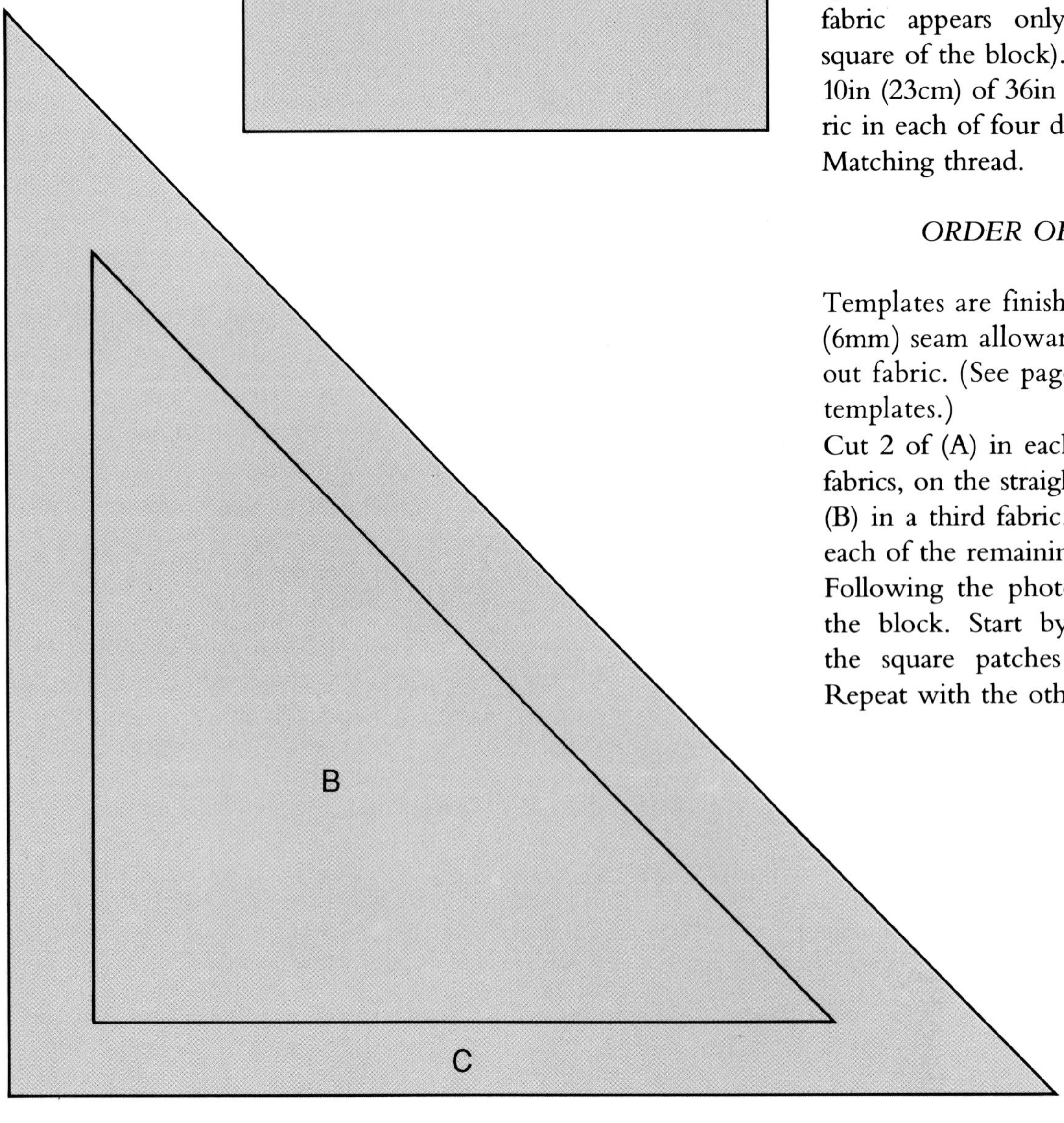

Size
Block 12in (30cm) square

MATERIALS

Five different, checked and striped cotton fabrics as follows: small piece approximately 8×4in (20×10cm) (this fabric appears only in the central square of the block).
10in (23cm) of 36in (90cm) wide fabric in each of four designs.
Matching thread.

ORDER OF WORK

Templates are finished size. Add ¼in (6mm) seam allowance when cutting out fabric. (See page 109 for making templates.)
Cut 2 of (A) in each of the first two fabrics, on the straight grain. Cut 4 of (B) in a third fabric. Cut 2 of (C) in each of the remaining fabrics.
Following the photograph, make up the block. Start by sewing two of the square patches together. Press. Repeat with the other two squares.

A

B

C

Join together to make up the central square of the block. Press.

Sew a piece (B) to two opposite sides of the square. Sew the remaining (B) pieces to the other two sides. Press. This makes a larger square.

Repeat with the (C) patches. This completes the block.

NOTE When cutting out right-angled triangles for blocks the rule is to have the sides adjacent to the right angle on the straight grain (see page 106). This rule has been broken here to make use of particular fabric patterns and so the othe side of the triangle has been placed on the straight grain.

This cushion, inspired by Samuel and Matilda Ross's quilt on page 79, follows the checks and stripes theme of the original, but the colours are bolder, dramatic reds, greys and black

TUMBLING
BLOCKS

The design known as Tumbling Blocks, Baby Blocks or the Box pattern was a favourite on both sides of the Atlantic throughout the nineteenth century. Originally used as an all-over design or border pattern for bedcovers, it was later made up into a variety of domestic furnishings, including cushions, curtains, chair seats and footstools.

It is made from three diamonds which together form a hexagon. When three different fabrics, often a dark, a medium and a light colour, are used, the illusion of a three-dimensional block is created. When repeated over an area the appearance is of a whole stack of blocks rather like children's building bricks. This design was used also as a quilting pattern.

An alternative pattern can be made by using six of the diamonds in a single fabric to form a star. Fabrics might be silk, velvet, cotton or woollen cloth, depending on the object being made and the taste and resources of the maker.

The footstool shown here was made from military uniforms. This fabric was used for a good deal of patchwork in the Victorian era – much of it worked by soldiers. This was not made by a soldier but by a daughter of the regiment. Nellie Bonnett, who came from an Indian Army family, made this stool in the 1880s from the uniforms of officers killed in the Indian Mutiny.

The design has been cleverly worked out to make the most of the dramatic black, red, white, blue and grey colouring. On the top, the box pattern radiates from a central six-point star. The boxes along the top and bottom edges of the stool have two dark sides which make a strong border and the star pattern reappears on the two short edges. The side panels feature diagonal stripes of diamonds with white used to separate and define the strong lines of red and blue.

Opposite: Nellie Bonnett's footstool, made in the 1880s from soldier's uniforms. The firm, felty wool proved a hard-wearing choice, although now showing signs of age

HEXAGONAL TABLECLOTH

The fact that each box or block of the Tumbling Blocks pattern is a hexagon inspired the shape of this cloth. It is usual to work this design using the English method but it can be worked by the American method if you prefer (see page 110).

Size

30in (76cm) diameter; each of the six sides measures 15in (38cm)

MATERIALS

½yd (45cm) of 45in (114cm)-wide silky fabric in each of three colours, blue, black and aubergine
Matching thread
Thin card (for the English method)
3¼yds (3m) of black bobble fringe

ORDER OF WORK

The templates are finished size. Cut papers from thin card. Add ¼in (6mm) seam allowance when cutting out fabric. (See page 109–110 for making templates and cutting papers.)
Using template (A) and with two sides on the straight grain, cut out 44 shapes in each colour.
Using template (B) and with one short side on the straight grain, cut out 8 shapes in each colour. (If the fabric has a pattern, such as a 'watered silk' effect, make sure the design lies in the same direction on each piece.)
Make up the cloth, following the illustration below, using three (A) shapes – one in each colour – for the boxes. Complete the design with (B) shapes as appropriate.

Opposite: Silk, satin and velvet was frequently chosen for the Tumbling Blocks pattern and here it is used for a hexagonal-shaped tablecloth in silky fabrics, edged with a Victorian-looking bobble fringe

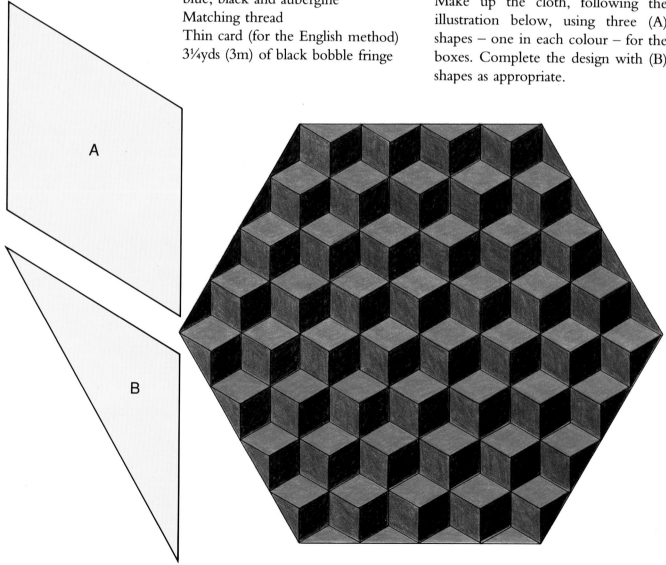

LONG DIAMOND

Ashape frequently seen in Victorian patchwork is the long diamond with angles of 45 and 135 degrees. This can be made up into an eight-point star. There are many nineteenth-century quilts which have several hundreds of small long diamonds making up one huge eight-point star as a central motif. In Britain this design is known simply as Star but in North America, where more evocative and romantic names are used for patchwork, it is known as Star of Bethlehem and Lone Star.

The diamond is equally attractive when positioned in a simple lattice pattern. When brightly coloured silk is used the effect is of a stained glass window.

At the beginning of the nineteenth century, small articles in diamond patchwork were often the work of children as the careful stitching needed to work accurate corners was considered good practice for plain sewing. One little girl made a set of velvet antimacassars in diamond pattern 'from ballgowns of the landed gentry'. Velvet would have been a difficult fabric to work, even for an adult, so her achievement is all the more notable. As the century progressed and patchwork became a pastime for the middle and upper classes, ladies addicted to fancy-work made seat covers, footstools, tea cosies, and even trimmed clothing with patchwork. They continued to make warm patchwork quilts and comforters for the poor, however, recycling worn-out clothing, and encouraged the less fortunate to apply themselves to this useful craft.

There is not much call for antimacassars these days – an evening bag made up of small brightly-coloured silk diamonds or a harlequin cushion in different-sized diamonds of silky fabrics might be rather more useful, and attractive things to make from patchwork.

The star motif was considered a symbol of good luck and fertility in the north of England, where this quilt was made around 1870. The huge central star of long diamonds and the smaller stars spinning from it were appliquéd to the background fabric by sewing machine although the quilting is worked by hand

EVENING BAG

The bag is made from long diamonds in six jewel colours, framed with black velvet to add impact to the design. To help give the silk stability and to emphasize the shapes, the work has been quilted along the seams. Work long diamonds using the english method (see page 110).

Size
Patchwork measures approximately 5¼in×6¾in (13.3×17cm)

MATERIALS

Scraps of silk in six colours
Matching threads
Thin card

ORDER OF WORK

Templates are finished size. Cut papers from thin card. Add ¼in (6mm) seam allowance when cutting out fabric. (See pages 109–110 for making templates and cutting papers.)
Using template (A), cut out 5 red, 4 pink, 3 green, 2 blue, 2 gold and 2 maroon pieces, with two sides on the straight grain.
Using template (B), cut out 1 red, 1 pink, 1 blue and 1 gold piece, with one short side on the straight grain.
Using template (C), cut out 2 green, 3 blue, 2 gold and 2 maroon pieces, with one long side on the straight grain.
Using template (D), cut out 1 green and 1 maroon piece, with the longest side on the straight grain.
Make up following the pattern.

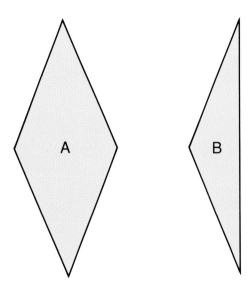

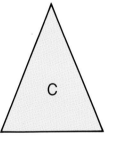

Opposite: The bright jewel colours used for this drawstring evening bag are enhanced by the 'frame' of black velvet. In true Victorian tradition, the bag is made from scraps of fabric

Follow the diagram below to assemble the diamonds and triangles for the evening bag

HARLEQUIN CUSHION

Four different coloured silk fabrics have been used to make up this design. It consists entirely of long diamonds in a progression of sizes. The centre of the pattern is four small diamonds, sewn together to make a larger diamond. This central diamond is then surrounded by eight more of the same size, making a nine-patch long diamond. The panel is completed with four triangles which together make up into a long diamond, again nine times bigger than the one just completed. As for the Evening bag, use the English method (see page 110).

Size
Patchwork measures approximately 8×15in (20×38cm)

MATERIALS

8in (20cm) square each of four different colours of silk
16in (40cm) square each of two of the colours (to complete a 15in (38cm) square cushion)

ORDER OF WORK

Templates given here, two diamonds and a right-angled triangle, are finished size. Cut papers from thin card. Add ¼in (6mm) seam allowance when cutting out fabric.
Using template (A), cut out 1 piece in each of the four colours, with two sides of the diamond on the straight grain.
Using template (E), cut out 2 pieces in each colour, with two sides of the diamond on the straight grain.
Using template (F), cut out 1 piece in each colour, with the sides adjacent to the right angle on the straight grain.
Make up the patchwork following the photograph opposite.

C

A

B

This harlequin cushion design is a more complex version of the one used for the bag on page 88. Only four colours have been used.

GRANDMOTHER'S FAN

A wide variety of different block patterns are based on the fan shape, such as Friendship Fan, Fanny's Fan and Imperial Fan. Probably the best known is the one featured on this delightful nineteenth-century piece, Grandmother's Fan.

Although most of the patchwork and quilting done in the nineteenth century was made up into bed covers, there were also a lot of table covers, carriage rugs and throws made. This piece (right) is a throw and would probably have been used on a sofa or draped over a piano. It was made in the early 1880s by a Pennsylvania Dutch (Deutsch) woman, Ellen Rimert of Northumberland County, Pennsylvania, USA.

The throw was made by hand, with all the pieces being cut without a template and some of the squares are not true. Once the top had been pieced, Ellen appears to have gone to town with the embroidery, outlining every seam, using a whole variety of stitches, including flag stitch, variegated coral, picot and feather stitches. At first glance the design looks more like an example of Crazy patchwork than Grandmother's Fan.

The top is fine wool chalice and the backing is cotton satin with a filling between the two layers. The quilting is purely utilitarian, serving just to hold the three layers together, with the stitching outlining the outer edge of each fan and square block. The throw, like many pieces of the time, is edged with a frill.

The fan blocks for the throw are assembled in fours, with two diagonally opposite ones placed together and the other two reversed. Like a great many block patterns, however, a single Grandmother's Fan block can stand alone. On page 95, one block has been used for the front of a workbag. Trace-off templates are given to work the patchwork.

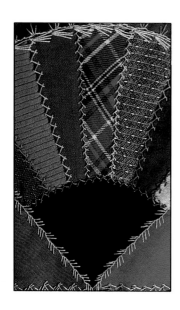

This throw was made entirely by hand, the pieces having been cut out without using templates thus the fans vary slightly in size.

WORK BAG

Soft, dress weight wool/cotton mixture fabrics in warm, rich colours have been chosen to give this bag a period feel, but you can use cotton fabrics if you prefer.

Make up this design using the American method, by hand or with a sewing machine (see page 110). Strips of plain fabric were added to the sides. (The amounts of fabric given will make up two sides of the bag.)

Size
Block measures 11½in (29cm) square.

MATERIALS

Wool/cotton mixture fabrics in the following colours and amounts:
¼yd (23cm) of 45in (114cm) wide plain dark red
¼yd (23cm) of 45in (114cm) wide plain dark green
7×12½in (18×32cm) dark red patterned fabric
6½×3in (16.5×7.5cm) navy patterned fabric
6½×3in (16.5×7.5cm) purple patterned fabric
6½×3in (16.5×7.5cm) green patterned fabric
Matching thread

Opposite: Fabrics in rich, warm colourings and traditional patterns give a period feel to this modern workbag. Unlike the throw on page 93, the pieces of the block have been outlined with quilting rather than with embroidery stitches.

ORDER OF WORK

Templates are finished size. Add ¼in (6mm) seam allowance when cutting fabric, placing one straight edge of each template on the straight grain.

Using template (A) cut out pieces in patterned fabrics as follows: 4 red, 1 navy, 1 purple, 1 green.

Using template (B), cut 1 plain red.

Using template (C), cut 1 plain red. Reverse the template and cut 1 plain green. (This gives two mirror image corner sections.)

Make up the block, following the photograph. Sew the pieces (A) of the fan together and press. Then sew the completed fan shape to piece (B) and press. Sew the two corner (C) sections together and press. Sew the outer edge of the fan to the corner section. Press.

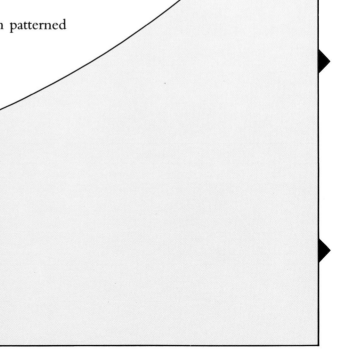

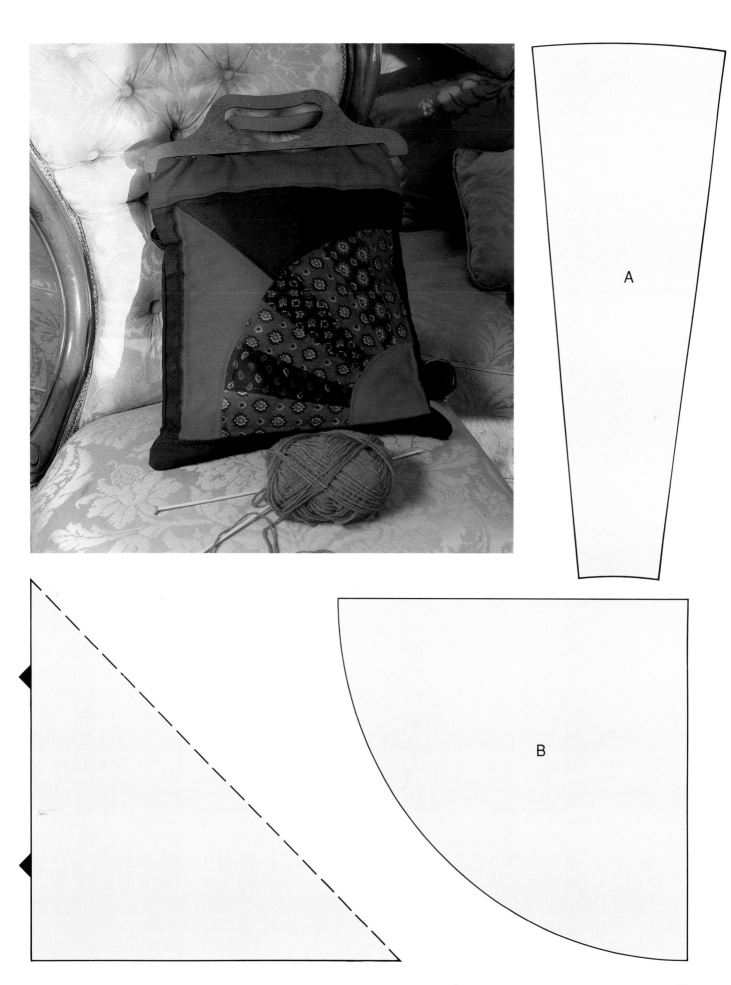

A

B

EIGHT-POINT STAR

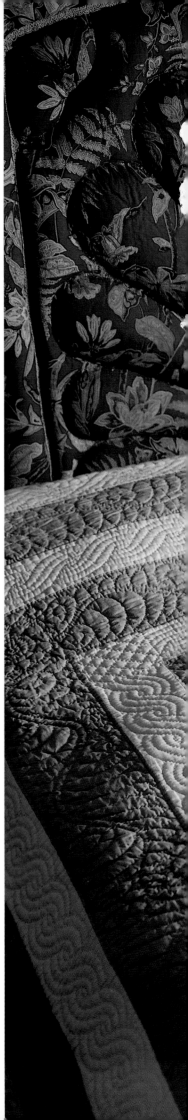

T his Eight-point Star pattern is really two stars – one superimposed on the other, made up into a square block. The design features, as a large central motif surrounded by plain borders, on a number of north of England quilts. The simple and bold colouring – pink and white, red and white, blue and white – gives maximum impact and shows off quilting to great advantage.

In the last century there were numerous women in the north of England who quilted for a living, and some who marked out the quilting pattern on quilt tops for others to work. The most famous was quilt 'stamper' Elizabeth Sanderson of Allenheads, Northumberland, who began her working life in the 1890s and continued until her death in the 1930s. This district was noted for its quilting designs and Miss Sanderson's quilt tops, and those of other local stampers, were sold through co-operative shops (jointly owned by many members – in this case local customers – who shared any profits) and by travelling salesmen over a wide area.

The Eight-point Star design, however, does not need to be quilted to be successful.

Opposite: The plain colours and simplicity of the Eight-point Star (detail on right) gave ample scope for the creative flair of the stamper and the expertise of the quilter. A popular patchwork design in Victorian times, a number of such quilts survive in varying colour schemes

EIGHT-POINT STAR STOOL

Firmly-woven lightweight furnishing cotton in two, clear, colours has a timeless effect. Work the design by hand using the American method (see page 110).

Size

Block measures 15¾in (40cm) square
Diameter of top of stool is approximately 17in (43cm)

MATERIALS

¼yd (23cm) of 48in (122cm)-wide cotton fabric, in yellow
¼yd (23cm) of 48in (122cm)-wide cotton fabric, in pale grey
NOTE To complete a footstool with a piped edge you will need ½yd (45cm) of yellow fabric and 1yd (90cm) of grey.
Matching thread

The star-within-a-star design works best as a single image on a piece of work, whether on a full-sized quilt like the one on page 97, a cushion, or on a footstool. Yellow has been teamed with grey here, instead of the traditonal white.

ORDER OF WORK

Templates on the opposite page, A, B, C, Ci and D, are finished size. Add ¼in (6mm) seam allowance when cutting fabric, placing one edge of each template on the straight grain. Use templates (C) and (D) for a square block; use template (Ci) for a round stool top or cushion. (See page 109 for making templates.)
Using template (A) cut out 8 grey pieces.
Using template (B) cut out 8 yellow pieces.
Using (C) cut out 4 grey pieces.
Using (D) cut out 4 grey pieces.
Or using (Ci) instead of (C) and (D) cut out 8 grey pieces.
Following the photograph below for the complete block, make up the patchwork.

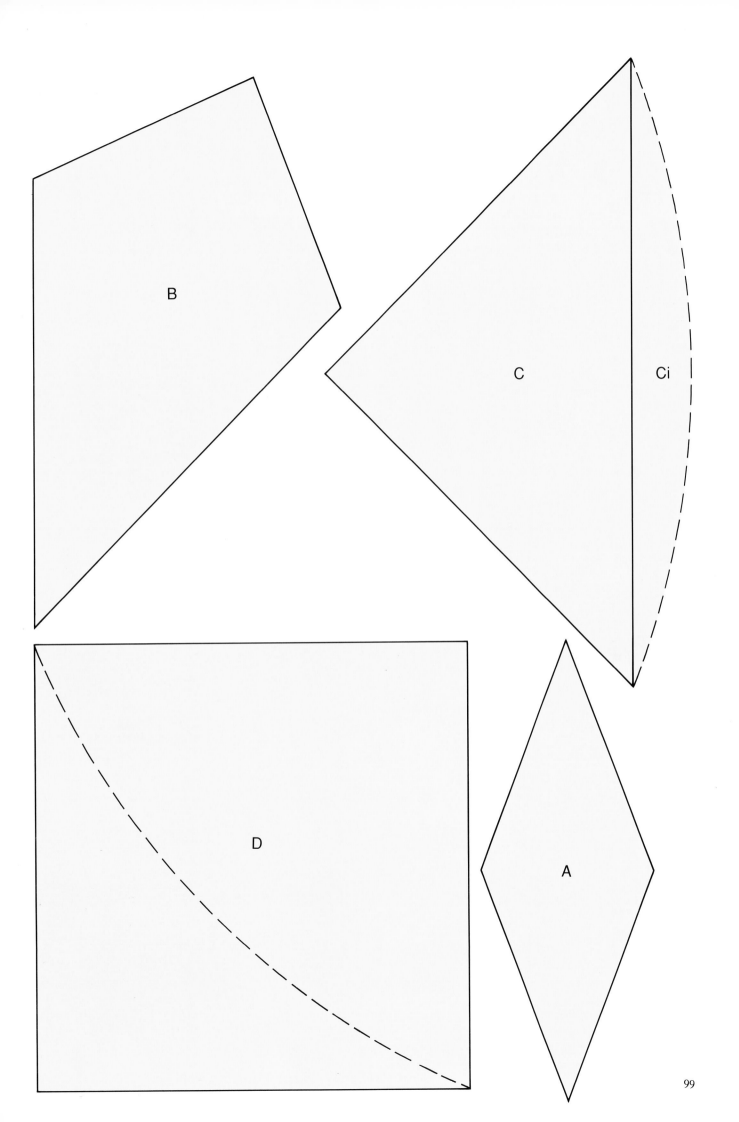

99

NINE-PATCH

Patchwork was originally developed when money and fabric were scarce, and every last scrap had to be used (and reused) to the best advantage. A quilt made today from rag-bag scraps would fit into this tradition of thrift and the simplest way to create it is to sew squares of fabric together until you have made up a large enough piece of cloth for the purpose in mind.

This very simple shape, however, has been used to create a whole range of interesting patterns. One way is to arrange squares in two colours, to give a cross of one colour on a background of another – the design is called Nine-Patch in the United States. Alternatively, three colours can be used, with the third being used as the centre of the cross.

The quilt on the right is based on this arrangement, but the squares have been arranged to give diagonal crosses. The pattern has then been extended to give a double border around the crosses. This quilt was made at the turn of the century from carefully-chosen remnants of flannels and suiting by Sybil Heslop, a farmer's wife from Northumberland in the north of England.

The frilled crib quilt on pages 102–104 made recently for a much-loved granddaughter, uses the same basic Nine–Patch cross design. This time, however, the squares are the conventional way up. making upright crosses.

Another way to arrange blocks of Nine-Patch is to alternate them with blocks of one of the colours to make a simple version of the design known as Irish Chain. The quilt on page 105 is another version of this pattern in which the block is made up of a central square surrounded by four rectangles and four smaller squares. The quilt was made in the latter part of the last century by a Cumbrian woman, Ada Elizabeth Robinson, and is still being used by a descendant today.

Opposite: The basic design of this turn-of-the-century quilt is a repeat pattern of diagonal crosses, each bordered with a different colour, with the whole design outlined with black. The design is symmetrical, based around a central upright cross

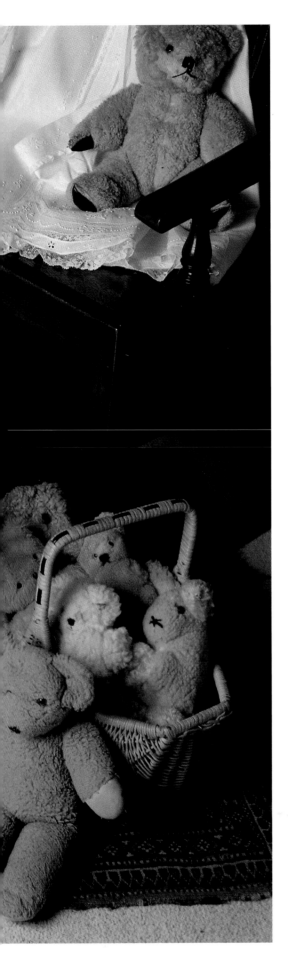

CRIB QUILT IN SQUARES

The design is of 12 block of nine small squares each, bordered with narrow strips to make larger squares which are in turn separated by narrow strips. The quilt is bordered with more strips and edged with broderie anglaise. It is decorated with embroidery. Make up this design using the American method (see page 110).

Size
The finished quilt measures approximately 21in×29in (55×77cm), plus frill

MATERIALS

The following amounts of 36in (90cm)- wide fabrics:
½yd (45cm) of pink, all-over mini-print (P1)
½yd (45cm) of blue, all-over mini-print (B1)
⅛yd (11.5cm) of paler pink all-over mini-print (P2)
⅛yd (11.5cm) of paler blue all-over mini-print (B2)
⅛yd (11.5cm) each of 4 different floral mini-prints (M1, M2, M4, M5)
¼yd (23cm), of two more floral mini-print (M3, M6)
⅛yd (11.5cm) of rabbit print (B3)
4yd (3.6m) of 1¾in (4.5cm)-wide broderie anglaise
Matching thread
Pink and blue stranded embroidery thread.

ORDER OF WORK

No templates are given for this design as it is made up entirely of squares and strips. The squares are 1½in (4cm) and you should make templates to this size. Add ¼in (6mm) seam allowance when cutting fabric (see page 109).

This delicately patterned quilt, in a variety of prints, with its recurring cross motif, is composed of small squares which together form a nine-patch block. The quilt is traditionally Victorian in style.

A seam allowance of ¼in (6mm) is included on the strips.

Using the template, cut out the following squares with all sides on the straight grain: B2, 24; P2, 24; M1, 12; M2, 12; M3, 12; M4, 12; B3, 12.

Following the single block diagram, and using B2, B3, M1 and M2, join the first nine squares together to make a mainly blue block. Press.

Make up five more blocks in the same way.

Outline each centre square with chain stitch using two strands of stranded embroidery thread.

Repeat with P2, B3, M3 and M4 to make six mainly pink blocks.

Cut the following from fabric P1: 12 strips 1¼×5in (31mm×13.2cm); 12 strips 1¼×6½in (31mm×17cm).

Sew one of the shorter strips to the top, and another to the bottom, of one of the pink blocks. Press. Sew a longer strip to each of the other two sides. Press.

Using two strands of stranded embroidery thread, work feather stitch (see page 66) over the join to outline the Nine-Patch block Repeat with the other five pink blocks.

Cut the same number and size of strips from fabric B1 and repeat the process with the blue blocks.

Cut 15 6½×1¼in (17×31mm) strips from M5.

Following the whole quilt diagram, make up three bands of four squares with lattice strips between the squares and at each end. Press.

Cut four strips of M3, 28¼×1¼in (74×31cm) wide. Join the bands together using these lattice strips. Sew another strip down each long side. From M6, cut 2 strips 21½×1¼in (56.2cm×31mm) and 2 strips 29¾×1¼in (79cm×31mm). Sew the two shorter strips along the top and bottom. Press. Then sew the two longer ones to the sides. Press.

If you wish, add chain stitch crosses in pink or blue, using two strands of stranded embroidery thread, at the corners of borders and intersections of lattice strips.

Make up into a quilt and trim with broderie anglaise.

Below: Follow the top diagram to construct the pink blocks. The lower diagram shows the arrangement for the blue blocks. The diagram to the right shows the complete quilt layout

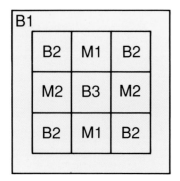

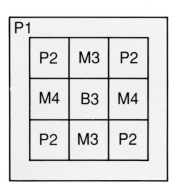

This is one of the many versions of the Irish Chain pattern which appears on quilts on both sides of the Atlantic. It is also known as Puss in the Corner. This quilt, from Cumbria in the north of England, is made from two cotton fabrics, a pink all-over print and a white and blue print. The design is made from 7in (18cm) blocks of 5 pink squares and 4 white rectangles, arranged like a checkerboard with 7in (18cm) squares. The quilt is bordered in pink fabric, diamond quilted.

TECHNIQUES

There are not many rules in patchwork. Different people work in different ways and 'right' and 'wrong' do not really apply. In general, use the way of working that suits you best.

The essential rule, however, is accuracy and this applies to all stages, from cutting templates to marking and stitching the fabric. Otherwise you can find yourself with all sorts of problems.

One of the joys of the craft is its adaptability. As you become more accustomed to doing patchwork and progress from the smaller articles to the larger tablecloth and quilts in this book, you will probably want to make your own templates and create your own designs. By following the techniques in this chapter, you will be assured of success in this absorbing and satisfying hobby.

FABRICS

Firmly-woven fabrics are the best for patchwork – dress-weight cottons, wool and cotton mixtures, fine wools, silks and velvets. The last two are more difficult to work with, but can be used to stunning effect.

In any one piece of work, use fabrics of similar weight so that they will wear evenly – usually all cottons or all wools. With some techniques, such as Log Cabin, similar weights are not so critical because the pieces are mounted on to a foundation fabric which compensates for slight differences. Dissimilar fabrics can also be used for Crazy patchwork because this is usually used for smaller, decorative items and part of its charm is the variety of fabrics chosen.

In addition, if an item is quilted this will stabilize the patchwork and will also make it more hardwearing.

It is acceptable – and very traditional – to recycle fabrics for patchwork. On the whole, however, it is best not to mix old and new fabrics in one piece of work. The old pieces will wear out more quickly than the new and the new, stronger, fabrics will tend to pull away from the old ones, causing the seams to fray.

Straight grain: Cut out patches with at least one edge on the straight grain of the fabric. When cutting fabrics for blocks, ensure that sides adjacent to right angles are on the straight grain, e.g. cut right-angled triangles with two short sides on the straight grain. This is necessary to ensure a good shape when making up the block. It is particularly important to have all four outer edges of the block on the straight grain.

Sometimes, as in the case of the cushion made from squares and triangles on page 22 you may decide to break the rule to make a particular use of a fabric. However, this is not advisable when making up a large piece of work.

EQUIPMENT

Patchwork does not require much in the way of tools and equipment and you probably already have most of them in your sewing box. There are, however, various aids to marking and cutting out which you may want to invest in if you intend to do a lot of patchwork.

All types of patchwork can be sewn by hand but where straight seams or gradual curves are involved, it is possible, and often preferable, to use a sewing machine.

NEEDLES: For hand sewing, everyone has their own favourites but, in general, choose a needle as fine and as short as you can comfortably work with.

In Victorian times, drapers' shops sold clothing, boots and shoes as well as bedlinens, fabrics and haberdashery. In shops like this, women could buy all they needed for quiltmaking, from needles and thread to fabrics and wadding

A piece of patchwork like this relies for its success on choosing just the right area of a fabric design. A window template makes this task easy

THREAD: Pure cotton thread is best as synthetic fibres tend to stretch in sewing.

When working by hand choose the thread colour to suit the patches being joined. If you are sewing a light patch to a darker, match the thread to the darker colour as dark on light is less obtrusive then light on dark.

When machine sewing, it is a nuisance to be continually changing thread, so pick a colour which predominates in the work.

PINS: Use fine pins – those sold as 'Wedding and Lace Pins' are ideal – to avoid marking the fabric. For the same reason, do not leave pins in the work longer than is absolutely necessary.

PENCILS AND RULERS: Use an ordinary lead pencil for drawing out templates and marking fabric. On some fabrics a coloured pencil may be better for contrast and in such cases choose either blue or yellow. You will also need a metal ruler when drawing out templates.

SCISSORS: Have three pairs of scissors for patchwork: good dressmaking scissors for cutting fabric, a small pair of embroidery scissors for trimming thread ends etc. and a separate pair of scissors for cutting patchwork papers from thin card.

CUTTING BOARD AND CRAFT KNIFE: These are useful for cutting papers and essential if you are making your own templates.

SANDPAPER: Fine sandpaper is invaluable for smoothing the edges of home-made templates.

TEMPLATES

There are two types of templates used for patchwork. Solid templates are used for marking out fabric and for cutting papers (Fig 1). Window templates are used for positioning patches on a specific area and for cutting fabric (Fig 2).

Although it is not essential to use a window template this is a very useful aid for cutting the fabric accurately and for selecting the exact part of a fabric design you wish to use. A window template is the same shape as the solid one, but is ¼in (6mm) larger all round, to include the seam allowance. It is also see-through in the centre (i.e., only the ¼in (6mm) border is solid).

MAKING YOUR OWN TEMPLATE: It is quite simple to make your own templates using the trace-off shapes in this book. They can be made from thick card or, if you intend to use the shape often, from see-through plastic. The latter is sold in sheets, either plain or marked with a grid.

If you are using card, accurately trace off the template you require, using a sharp pencil and a ruler. Paste the tracing on to card and cut out, using a craft knife, ruler and cutting board. Smooth the edges with sandpaper. If you are using plastic, lay this over the appropriate template pattern and trace off and then cut out.

It is a good idea to make a window template for each shape in your patchwork. Draw round the solid template on a piece of card. Draw another line all around ¼in (6mm) from the first. Using a craft knife and ruler and a cutting board, cut away the centre shape, then cut around the outer line. Smooth the edges with sandpaper.

BOUGHT TEMPLATES: Ready-made templates can be obtained in a wide range of sizes and shapes. They are usually sold in sets of a solid metal template and a plastic window template.

The solid template is used for cutting papers and for marking out fabric

The window template enables the exact area of fabric to be chosen and includes a ¼in (6mm) seam allowance for cutting fabric

PAPERS

These are used for working the English method of sewing patchwork. Although they are known as 'papers' they should not be cut from notepaper or the pages of a magazine. These are far too thin and pliable and can cause inaccuracies in the work. Greetings cards, however, are ideal. They are the right weight to ensure accuracy and make sewing easy.

Papers may be cut with scissors or with a craft knife and cutting board, whichever you find easiest.

It is sometimes said that one should never pencil round the template before cutting out papers, but should hold the template firmly against the card and cut out with the blade of the scissors hard up against the template. It is, however, acceptable to draw round if the pencil point is very sharp. Angle the pencil into the template so the line is absolutely accurate.

Never cut some papers one way and some another in the same piece of work. You will get differences in sizes which will lead to trouble at the joining stage.

SEWING TECHNIQUES

Basically, there are two different methods of making up patchwork, with and without papers. The first technique, known as the English method, is always sewn by hand. The second, known as the American method, can be worked by hand or by sewing machine.

English method
This is used for almost any shape of patch. Use a window template to mark the cutting line on the wrong side of the fabric. (There is no need to mark out the sewing line as you are using the papers to make the shape.) Cut out the shape. Place a paper centrally on the wrong side of the fabric shape and pin the two together (Fig 1). Fold over the seam allowance and baste in place, paying particular attention to the corners (Fig 2). Wide-angled shapes are the easiest to work with; sharp angled ones are a little more difficult (Fig 3).

To join two patches together, place them right sides together. Knot the thread end and begin just in from the corner. Oversew along the edge to be joined with tiny stitches taken on the very edge of the fold, sewing back towards the corner before working along the seam. End by stitching back along the seam for a short distance (Fig 4). The weakest point of this type of patchwork is where three shapes meet. To lessen the problems, never stitch along more than two adjacent sides without fastening off the thread end. It also helps to reinforce corners with a few extra stitches. For the same reason, it is advisable to leave the papers in place until the whole patchwork is completed.

American method
This is the ideal technique for block patterns which usually involve only straight seams.
HAND SEWING: Papers are not used with this technique. Mark both the cutting and sewing lines on the wrong side of the fabric making sure that the sewing lines are absolutely accurate.

Place two patches right sides together and pin (Fig 5). Knot the thread end and work two or three back stitches, then sew along the seam with small running stitches, making a back stitch every few stitches. Finish with back stitches (Fig 6). Sew from raw edge to raw edge.
NOTE If you are joining shapes which involve working round corners (i.e., the Eight-Point Star design on page 96), take the seam along the sewing line only.

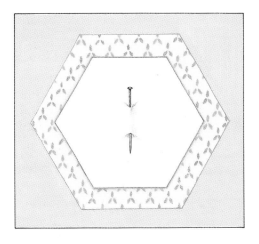

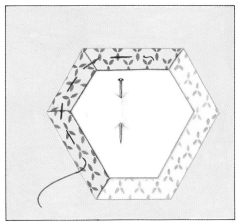

Pin the paper shape centrally to the fabric shape

Fold the seam allowance on to the paper and baste in place

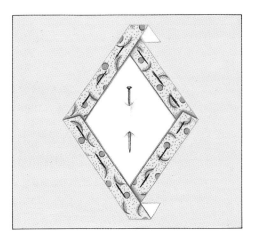

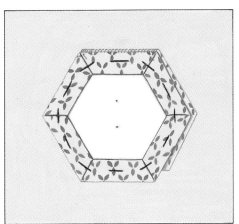

When working diamond patches, the corners need to be folded twice

Oversew patches together, right on the fold, taking tiny stitches through the fabric only

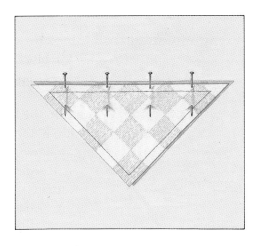

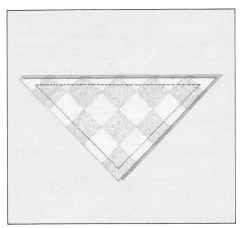

In the American method, patches are pinned together right sides facing

Patches are then joined with small running stitches, with a back stitch worked every few stitches

MACHINE SEWING: This is worked in the same way as for the hand method, but using a medium-length straight machine stitch.

There is an alternative way to work by machine, but the fabric must be very accurately cut. In this method there is no need to mark the sewing line. Simply use the width of the machine foot as a guide. (It must be exactly ¼in (6mm) wide, or you can mark the foot plate with masking tape ¼in (6mm) from the needle hole as a guide.)

Pressing

It is important to press seams as they are completed. Press seams open or to one side. If you intend to quilt the work along the seam the latter method is preferable.